Inflation Targeting in Practice

Strategic and Operational Issues and Application to Emerging Market Economies

Editors
Mario I. Blejer
Alain Ize
Alfredo M. Leone
Sergio Werlang

International Monetary Fund

Cover design and figures: Luisa Menjivar-Macdonald
Typesetting: Alicia Etchebarne-Bourdin

Library of Congress Cataloging-in-Publication Data

Inflation targeting in practice : strategic and operational issues and application to
   emerging market economies / editors, Mario I. Blejer . . . [et al.].
      p. cm.
   Includes bibliographical references.
   ISBN 1-55775-889-1
   1. Inflation (Finance)—Government policy—Case studies. 2. Monetary policy—
Case studies. I. Blejer, Mario I. II. International Monetary Fund.

   HG229.I4567 2000   00-035115
   332.4'15—dc21   CIP

Price: $24.50

Address orders to:
International Monetary Fund, Publication Services
700 19th Street, N.W., Washington, D.C. 20431, U.S.A.
Tel.: (202) 623-7430   Telefax: (202) 623-7201
E-mail: publications@imf.org
Internet: http://www.imf.org

recycled paper

Contents

Contributors

Claes Berg is Chief Economist in the Economics Department of the Sveriges Riksbank.

Mario I. Blejer is Senior Advisor in the Asia and Pacific Department at the International Monetary Fund.

Gil Bufman is Lecturer at the Academic College of Tel-Aviv Yaffo and a private economic consultant.

Agustín G. Carstens is Executive Director at the International Monetary Fund.

Guy Debelle is Deputy Head of the Economic Analysis Department at the Reserve Bank of Australia.

Marvin Goodfriend is Senior Vice President and Director of Research at the Federal Reserve Bank of Richmond.

Andrew Haldane is Head of International Finance at the Bank of England.

Alain Ize is Advisor in the Monetary and Exchange Affairs Department at the International Monetary Fund.

Leonardo Leiderman is Senior Director of the Research Department at the Bank of Israel and Professor of Economics at the Berglas School of Economics at Tel-Aviv University.

Alfredo M. Leone is Chief, Financial Systems Surveillance Division I, in the Monetary and Exchange Affairs Department at the International Monetary Fund.

David Longworth was, at the time of the conference, Chief of the Research Department of the Bank of Canada.

Felipe Morandé is Chief Economist at the Central Bank of Chile.

Klaus Schmidt-Hebbel is Chief of Economic Research at the Central Bank of Chile.

Murray Sherwin is Deputy Governor of the Reserve Bank of New Zealand.

Sergio Werlang is Deputy Governor of the Central Bank of Brazil.

Alejandro M. Werner is Director of Research at the Bank of Mexico.

Preface

In the aftermath of its resolution, in January 1999, to float the exchange rate of the real, the Central Bank of Brazil decided also to change the operational framework of its monetary policy and to adopt an explicit inflation targeting approach. In so doing, Brazil followed an increasing number of economies, both industrial and emerging, that have moved toward this type of arrangement. To inform the process of preparing for the introduction of the new scheme, the Central Bank of Brazil and the Monetary and Exchange Affairs Department of the International Monetary Fund held a seminar on inflation targeting in Rio de Janeiro on May 3–5, 1999. Its purpose was to analyze the experience to date of the countries that have been operating under an inflation targeting framework, and to identify and review the steps that Brazil should consider in adopting such a framework, to enhance the chances of its success.

Experts from 10 central banks joined their Brazilian counterparts and officials from the IMF in an in-depth examination of the recent experience, including practical aspects of the design and operation of inflation targeting in both industrial and emerging economies. A paper on the usefulness of inflation targeting in pursuing price stability and comprehensive papers on each of nine countries were presented and discussed. This volume gathers together the summaries of those presentations, which treat the main relevant points raised in the papers without entering into the most country-specific details. The objective is to present a concise but complete guide to the theoretical considerations and practical aspects that are important in assessing the benefits and costs of this increasingly popular monetary strategy.

The editors are grateful to the contributing authors for their efforts in preparing the concise versions of their papers, and to their colleagues at the Central Bank of Brazil and in the Monetary and Exchange Affairs Department and the Western Hemisphere Department of the IMF. They are also thankful to Nora Mori-Whitehouse for her efficient logistical and technical support in the preparation of this volume.

1   Introduction and Overview

Mario I. Blejer and Alfredo M. Leone

It is not an easy task to find many areas in economics where almost full agreement has emerged in the last few years. However, there is today a widespread and growing consensus that the single most important goal of monetary policy should be the pursuit of price stability. Reflecting this recognition, an increasing number of central banks have been granted independence and charged with the exclusive objective of controlling inflation and preserving the stability of prices. But embracing price stability as the explicit primary goal for monetary policy does not preclude the adoption of different operating mechanisms, and the choice of monetary regime that will best serve the objective of price stability has, indeed, generated much debate.

There are two basic persuasions on this matter, which boil down to the old debate over discretion versus rules. Those who believe in the superiority of policymaker discretion insist that, in practice, monetary policy tends to be largely judgmental. Although certain variables may be useful indicators of inflationary trends, policymakers fighting inflation look at a great many factors at the same time, interpret them in the manner that seems to them most correct, and decide on policies accordingly. Those who believe in rules, on the other hand, resolutely support the adoption of definite and precise targets—whether for growth in specific monetary aggregates, a level or path of the exchange rate, or a rate of inflation. The main argument for the adoption of targets is the notion that to conquer inflation, and thereafter to preserve price stability, requires policy credibility, and credibility, in turn, requires consistency, commitment, and transparency, which cannot be achieved without the accountability that arises from the adoption of explicit targets.

Although the debate remains unresolved, a growing number of countries have come out in favor of explicit rules. Among them, a significant number have chosen to eschew the growth path of a monetary aggregate as the explicit target for monetary policy. Instead they have decided to operate within a so-called *pure inflation targeting regime,* defined as the *public declaration of a quantitative target for inflation* in the medium run, coupled with a commitment by the central bank to pursue and reach this target. New Zealand was the first country to adopt this monetary strategy, but it was soon followed by a number of other industrial countries, among them Australia, Canada, Finland, Sweden, and the United Kingdom. More recently, several emerging economies have also moved in this direction, including Chile, Israel, Mexico, and in 1999, Brazil. Many other central banks are now actively considering the applicability of this regime to their countries, and some are making definite preparations to adopt the scheme.

One of the reasons why an explicit inflation targeting regime is so popular today is that it seems to lack some of the drawbacks of alternative monetary policy regimes. For example, the targeting of monetary aggregates—such as the monetary base or a broader measure of money—has a number of benefits, but in reality it is only advantageous when one can establish a high and predictable correlation between the chosen aggregate and nominal income. In fact, the demand for money has displayed strong fluctuations and frequent structural changes over time, rendering the relationship between the money supply (as reflected by the most relevant aggregate) and the policy objective (a particular level of inflation or of nominal income growth) highly unstable. Therefore the adoption of monetary aggregates as the target variable for monetary policy has become troublesome, and many countries have abandoned the practice and engaged in an active search for an alternative nominal anchor.

The other popular nominal anchor, particularly for small, open economies, has been the adoption of a preannounced (or at least predetermined) path for the exchange rate. Such an anchor may take the form of a fixed exchange rate regime (or even a currency board) or a crawling peg with well-defined rules for the crawl. Clearly, however, with the adoption of a fixed exchange rate rule, the central bank gives up the ability to control its own monetary policy and accepts limits on its capability to respond to domestic and external shocks. Moreover, as the recent financial crises in emerging economies have shown, fixed exchange rate regimes can suffer discrete breakdowns. The resulting violent changes in exchange rates may be extremely disruptive, not least because they can result in systemic banking and financial crises and broadly affect the level of economic activity.

It was this growing disappointment with quantity-based monetary policy, on the one hand, and the problems faced by many countries operating under an exchange rate rule, on the other, that induced some emerging economies to adopt—and many more to consider adopting—explicit inflation targeting. In particular, in emerging economies that are increasingly operating in a context of free capital mobility and liberalized financial markets, both monetary aggregates and the velocity of money have been rendered largely unstable. In addition, in time of crisis (such as in the Mexican crisis of 1994–95), the rule for money growth was often unable to prevent the sudden depreciation of the domestic currency, and therefore could not have the desired effect on inflationary expectations and the price level. As a result, the use of monetary targets as operational objectives was deemphasized. This is not to say that monetary aggregates were discarded altogether as policy indicators, but their prominence diminished significantly. Under these conditions, the adoption of an inflation target was seen as the most appropriate way of establishing and announcing to the public an explicit inflation objective, backed by a commitment to its attainment through supportive monetary policy.

In all the countries whose experiences are reviewed in this book, inflation targeting was adopted in the context of a move from a fixed (or predetermined) exchange rate toward a more flexible exchange rate regime, although the degree of flexibility varied across countries. In some cases a fixed exchange rate regime was replaced with a system of exchange rate bands, whereas in others a floating exchange rate system was adopted. Although the move to a more flexible exchange rate regime was seen as removing, or at least significantly moderating, one source of exogeneity in the behavior of monetary variables, in all cases the authorities were clearly concerned that the move could increase inflation expectations and result in inflationary pressures. Since low inflation continued to be recognized as the primary objective of monetary policy, the adoption of an inflation targeting framework was seen as key to anchoring expectations and guiding monetary policy decisions.

The Transition to Inflation Targeting

Prerequisites

The experience of several inflation targeters points to several prerequisites for successful adoption of an inflation targeting framework. First, the central bank must be given complete *instrument independence.* That is, it must have the freedom to adjust its instruments of monetary policy in the manner it believes will best achieve the objective of low inflation. Instrument independence mainly implies that the central bank is not constrained by the need to finance the government budget. Once all of the government's funding requirements are being met directly from private markets, another major exogenous influence on central bank liabilities is removed.

Second, the central bank must have an *effective monetary policy instrument*, one that has a relatively stable relationship with inflation. Most countries that have adopted inflation targeting use indirect instruments of monetary control, such as short-term interest rates, rather than direct instruments, such as credit controls.

Third, central bank independence under inflation targeting must be accompanied by *improved accountability, transparency, and communication with the public.* It is important to keep the public well informed about how the central bank operates and, in particular, about how new information causes the central bank to update its views of future prospects and to modify its policy stance. This is needed to ensure the public's understanding of the inflation target and its role as an anchor for inflation expectations. In many countries that have adopted an inflation targeting framework, central banks publish periodically an inflation report, which provides a flow of information and analysis that permits the central bank to explain its policy actions and to deflect accusations that could damage its credibility. Several other vehicles can be used to ensure accountability and transparency of monetary policy in these countries. One of these is the mandatory issuance by the central bank of an open letter, when the targets are breached, explaining the causes of the breach, the measures to be adopted to ensure that inflation returns to tolerated levels, and the period of time that will be needed for these measures to have an effect. Another is appearances of members of the central bank's governing body before parliamentary committees. A third is publication of the minutes of the meetings of the monetary policy committee that decides on interest rates.

Technical Issues

The country experiences summarized here also highlight several technical issues that any inflation targeting framework must address if it is to succeed. One of these is the selection of a *relevant price index* as the measure of inflation to target. Also, it must be decided whether to focus for policy purposes on an underlying or "core" measure of inflation, one that excludes certain more variable components of the price index adopted. If this is done, the authorities will need to provide clear definitions of and explanations for these exclusions before adopting the price index.

A decision will also need to be made on *whether to specify the inflation target as a point, as a band, or as a medium-term average;* the *time horizon* for meeting the target must be specified as well. In considering these alternatives, the authorities will need to take into account the trade-off between retaining some flexibility to deal with transitory inflationary impulses and providing a suitable and credible anchor for inflation expectations and policy decisions.

Most important, the authorities must have a clear target and be explicit about the definition of this target and the target horizon.

The monetary authorities must have a clear view about the *monetary policy transmission mechanism*. In particular, there should be a clear understanding of the roles of short-term interest rates, the exchange rate, and money and credit. They should also be aware of the major shocks that have typically affected aggregate demand and inflation in their country in the past. All these elements should be useful in identifying the channels that are most suitable for achieving the inflation target over time.

The authorities must be able to count on *reliable forecasts of inflation*. This is a key element, because the inflation targeting framework is necessarily forward-looking, given the lagged effects of any monetary policy action. Although it may not be essential at the outset to develop a reliable economic model of inflation that draws together all the relevant information and produces reliable forecasts, such a model is desirable in the long run.

In building *supporting models* to simulate the monetary transmission mechanism and produce inflation forecasts, the best advice is to keep these models small and simple, especially at first. Research should focus on small to medium-size models that embody the main features needed for the conduct of monetary policy. Most inflation targeters impose theoretical restrictions on these models when appropriate, as well as other suitable prior assumptions derived from smaller models and vector autoregressive (VAR) models.

However, in all cases it must be recognized that the use of models for economic projections is always supplemented by *judgment*. It is also important to monitor data that become available between projections, including data on variables that may not be included in the models but can help the authorities form a judgment on the path of inflation. These variables normally include monetary and credit aggregates, measures of the output gap, and measures of the public's inflation expectations.

Trade-offs

The experience so far with inflation targeting has brought to light a trade-off between flexibility and credibility. The more flexible the framework, the less credible it tends to be. The choice of a particular measure of the inflation rate (for instance, the use of an underlying or core measure), the adoption of measures to enhance credibility (including frequent and transparent communication with the public), and the choice of the policy horizon all affect this trade-off. Too much flexibility may undermine the public's confidence in the regime. But too much rigidity may result in unnecessarily large variability of output. The main message from the experience so far is the need to establish credibility as early as possible, to weaken the trade-off and thus allow greater flexibility in the longer run.

Under an inflation targeting framework, the monetary authorities can conceivably pursue additional objectives, *but only to the extent that they are consistent with the inflation target.* Experience to date clearly shows that the co-existence of multiple anchors (typically, a crawling currency band together with an inflation target, or a monetary aggregate target together with an inflation target) sooner or later becomes a source of policy conflict, which usually damages credibility.

The Plan of the Book

The experience of the countries surveyed in this volume seems to demonstrate that the adoption of explicit inflation targeting, and the way in which the choices for that framework have been made, have had an impact on the manner in which monetary policy was implemented and on the results observed. There has been no lack of variety in the design and implementation of inflation targeting strategies, and this variety has yielded some important insights on the consequences of alternative options.

This book can be analytically divided into three parts. The first, which consists of Chapter 2, is devoted to a discussion by Marvin Goodfriend of the reasons why inflation targeting is useful, in the context of an analysis of the importance and implications of pursuing the price stability objective.

The second part, comprising Chapters 3 through 7, examines the details of implementation of inflation targeting in five industrial countries. Although these chapters discuss many of the same analytical and practical issues, they also emphasize different aspects of inflation targeting according to the experience of each country. In Chapter 3, which presents the case of New Zealand—the inflation targeting pioneer—Murray Sherwin stresses the adoption of the new monetary framework as one of several overall strategic choices within a comprehensive reform program. On the other hand, the case of Sweden, as discussed by Claes Berg in Chapter 4, emphasizes the role of inflation targeting in dealing with uncertainty. The Canadian experience, as considered by David Longworth in Chapter 5, highlights the importance of specifying the transmission mechanism and of reliable inflation forecasts. The potential conflict between inflation targeting and the pursuit of other objectives, particularly output stabilization, is emphasized in Chapter 6, on Australia, by Guy Debelle, and the role of the institutional framework is highlighted in Andrew Haldane's discussion of the U.K. experience in Chapter 7.

The third part of the book, Chapters 8 through 11, deals with emerging economies and the ways in which inflation targeting has been adapted to their circumstances. Chapter 8, by Felipe Morandé and Klaus Schmidt-Hebbel, describes the Chilean experience and stresses the importance of regime credibility. The case of Israel, analyzed by Leonardo Leiderman and Gil Bufman in Chapter 9, points out the difficulties in switching from exchange rate to inflation targeting, whereas in Chapter 10, on Mexico, Agustín Carstens and Alejandro Werner focus on the role of inflation targeting in dealing with supply shocks. Finally, the case of Brazil, which adopted inflation targeting in mid-1999, is discussed in Chapter 11. Written by the research department of the Central Bank of Brazil, this final chapter focuses on the issues involved in planning and designing the introduction of inflation targeting.

Taken as a whole, the brief but wide-ranging discussions presented in this volume indicate that inflation targeting has been successful in many countries in reducing inflation and maintaining it at low levels—something that many of these same countries had failed to achieve in the past. In addition, the chapters present no evidence that the introduction of an inflation targeting framework has had unwanted consequences for the real economy beyond the very short run. Both these conclusions seem to apply to both industrial and emerging economies. Since inflation targeting offers a number of operational advantages and relatively few and manageable drawbacks, it indeed constitutes a monetary strategy that other countries should seriously study and further consider.

2   Maintaining Low Inflation: Rationale and Reality

Marvin Goodfriend[1]

Inflation targeting has emerged in recent years as the leading framework within which monetary policy is conducted around the world. In the United States, the Federal Reserve does not have an explicit inflation target, but it is fair to say that the Fed today, as never before in its history, is committed to maintaining low inflation. Likewise, the Bank of Japan is committed to maintaining stable prices, and the new Eurosystem has adopted an explicit target band for inflation in response to the price stability mandate in the Maastricht Treaty. Central banks in countries such as Australia, Canada, Israel, New Zealand, Sweden, and the United Kingdom today employ inflation targets.

The Costs of Inflation

The idea that central banks should give priority to price stability over economic growth and unemployment objectives has taken root gradually over a number of years, as a result of accumulated practical experience with inflation and theoretical advances in monetary economics. As a first approximation, it turns out that the lessons from theory and practice have been mutually supportive of the advantages of giving pride of place to a low-inflation objective for monetary policy.

The recommended priority for price stability derives not from any belief in its intrinsic value relative to growth and employment. Rather, price stability should take priority for two reasons: first, a central bank actually has the power to guarantee price stability over the long run, and second, monetary

---

[1]The views expressed are the author's alone and not necessarily those of the Federal Reserve Bank of Richmond or the Federal Reserve System.

policy encourages employment and economic growth in the long run mostly by controlling inflation. Also, and this is very important, an inflation target need not prevent a central bank from taking policy actions to stabilize financial markets and employment in the short run. It does, however, discipline a central bank to justify such actions against its commitment to protect the purchasing power of money.

The costs of inflation are significant and varied. A steady rate of inflation imposes a cost, but so does an unsteady, unpredictable rate of inflation. Understanding the cost of steady inflation begins with the fact that a steadily falling purchasing power of money causes people to hold less cash than they would if prices were stable. Attempts to economize on money holdings manifest themselves in several ways. Banks invest in more automated teller machines and faster processes for clearing checks, and people visit banks more frequently. People take more time and expense to protect the value of their savings and investments against loss due to inflation. The effort and resources devoted to dealing with inflation are wasted from society's point of view in the sense that they could be better employed producing goods and services.

Another major cost of steady inflation stems from the incomplete indexation of the tax system. The biggest problem in this regard, at least in the United States, results from the fact that taxes are assessed on nominal interest earnings and nominal capital gains, that is, on investment returns in dollars. Inflation causes nominal returns to rise because investors demand compensation for the declining purchasing power of money. For instance, long-term bond rates contain a premium for expected inflation over the life of the bond. But because nominal returns are taxed as income, inflation reduces the after-tax return to saving and investment and thereby tends to inhibit capital accumulation and economic growth.

The disruptive and destabilizing costs of unstable inflation are more difficult to quantify but are substantial nonetheless. These costs stem from the alternating expansionary and contractionary policy actions that tend to be associated with inflationary monetary policy. Some central banks, including the Federal Reserve in the past, have shown a tendency to engage in go-stop monetary policy, which accentuates rather than dampens the cyclical volatility of inflation and unemployment.

The Political Economy of Inflation: The Case of the Federal Reserve

For the most part, the U.S. public tolerated inflation as long as it was low, steady, and predictable. When labor markets were slack, they were even willing to risk higher inflation in order to stimulate additional economic activity. Only when economic activity was strong and inflation moved well above the prevailing trend did inflation top the list of public concerns.

It is easy to understand why inflation need not greatly concern the public when it is steady and predictable. Individuals and firms are inconvenienced only slightly by steady inflation. As long as wages, prices, and asset values move up in tandem, the financial consequences are modest, especially when inflation is low. Likewise, a temporary and modest increase in inflation around a low, well-established trend need not immediately arouse concerns.

However, a persistent departure of inflation above its trend causes anxieties, because people then wonder whether a new trend might be established. Investors worry about how much of an inflation premium to demand in interest rates; businesses worry about how aggressively to price their output in order to cover rising costs; workers worry about maintaining the purchasing power of their wages.

In marked contrast to inflation, which affects all, unemployment actually affects a relative few at any given time. In the United States in recent decades, the unemployment rate has risen at most to only about 10 percent of the labor force. People are concerned about unemployment not so much out of sympathy for those currently unemployed but because they are afraid of becoming unemployed themselves. It follows that the public is generally more concerned about unemployment when the unemployment rate is rising, even if it is still low, than when it is falling, even if it is already high.

This reasoning helps explain why the Fed produced go-stop monetary policy in the 1960s and 1970s. In retrospect, one observes the following pattern of events:

- Because inflation became a major concern only after it had clearly moved above its previous trend, the Fed did not tighten policy early enough to preempt inflationary outbursts before they became a problem.

- By the time the public had become sufficiently concerned about inflation to prompt the Fed to act, pricing decisions had already begun to embody higher inflation expectations. Thus delayed, a given degree of restraint on inflation required a more aggressive increase in short-term interest rates, with greater risk of recession.

- During each of these cyclical episodes there was a relatively narrow window of broad public support for the Fed to tighten monetary policy. The window would open after inflation was widely recognized to be a problem, and close when tighter monetary policy caused the unemployment rate to begin to rise. Often, the Fed did not take full advantage of these windows of opportunity to raise short-term rates because it wanted more confirmation that higher short-term rates were required.

• It was probably easier for the Fed to maintain public support for fighting inflation with prolonged tightening after inflation had emerged rather than with preemptive tightening. A more gradual lowering of short-term interest rates in the later stage of a recession was a less visible means of fighting inflation than raising rates more sharply earlier. Once unemployment had peaked and begun to fall, the public's anxiety about it diminished. Prolonged tightening was attractive as an inflation-fighting measure in spite of the fact that it probably lengthened the "stop" phase of the policy cycle.

Romer and Romer (1989) document that, since World War II, the Fed has tightened monetary policy decisively to fight inflation on six occasions, beginning in October 1947, September 1955, December 1968, April 1974, August 1978, and October 1979. The unemployment rate rose sharply during each "stop" phase of the policy cycle. Only two significant increases in unemployment during this period were not preceded by Fed action to fight inflation. The first occurred in 1954 after the Korean War and the second in 1961, after the Fed tightened monetary policy to improve the U.S. balance of payments.

Over time, workers and firms came to anticipate the Fed's deliberately expansionary monetary policy in the "go" phase of the policy cycle. Workers learned to take advantage of tight labor markets to make higher wage demands, and firms took advantage of tight product markets to pass along the higher costs in higher prices. Increasingly aggressive wage- and price-setting behavior tended to neutralize the favorable employment effects of expansionary policy. The Fed became ever more expansionary, on average, in its pursuit of low unemployment (even as the average unemployment rate tended to rise over time), causing correspondingly higher inflation and higher inflation expectations. Lenders demanded unprecedentedly high inflation premiums in long-term bond rates. The absence of a long-run anchor for inflation caused inflation expectations and long-term bond rates to fluctuate widely. For instance, the 30-year bond rate rose from around 8 percent in 1978 to peak above 14 percent in the fall of 1981.

The breakdown of mutual understanding between the markets and the Fed greatly inhibited the effectiveness of monetary policy. The Fed continued to closely manage short-term nominal interest rates. But the result of an interest rate policy action is largely determined by its effect on the real interest rate, which is the nominal rate minus the public's expected rate of inflation. The Fed found it increasingly difficult to estimate the public's inflation expectations and to predict how its policy actions might influence those expectations. Compounding the problem, enormous increases in short-term interest rates were required by the early 1980s to stabilize inflation. To sum up, stabilization policy became more difficult because the public could not predict what a given policy action implied for the future, and consequently, the Fed could not predict how the economy would respond to its policy actions.

Conducting monetary policy without a firmly established nominal anchor for the inflation rate opens a central bank to still another kind of risk. When there is no quantity or price constraint on monetary policy, and a central bank has shown its willingness to tolerate rising inflation over time, the public naturally becomes nervous about the possibility of future outbursts of inflation. Inflation "scares," which reflect a sudden, sharp rise in inflation expectations, can manifest themselves in a significant rise in long-term bond rates. A central bank that has not acted to defend a low inflation objective is particularly susceptible to a sudden loss of credibility for its claims to seek low inflation.

Inflation scares pose a difficult dilemma for a central bank. They are costly because resisting them requires the central bank to raise real short-term interest rates, with potentially depressing effects on business conditions. Hesitating is also costly, however, because it encourages workers and firms to ask for wage and price increases, to protect themselves from higher expected costs. The central bank is then inclined to accommodate the higher actual inflation with faster money growth. If the central bank lacks a track record for defending low inflation, inflation scares may be induced by any number of different factors, greatly complicating macroeconomic prediction and control.

The Importance of Being Credible: Lessons from the Fed's Success

The Fed has succeeded in maintaining low inflation for almost 15 years now. The challenge today is to understand the secret of that monetary policy success. In that regard, the recent period of low inflation has as much to teach as the traumatic period that preceded it.

One of the most important lessons learned is that credibility for low inflation is the foundation of effective monetary policy. The Fed has acquired credibility since the early 1980s by consistently taking policy actions to hold inflation in check. In effect, the Fed reestablished a mutual understanding between itself and the markets. From this perspective, wage and price setters keep their part of an implicit bargain by not raising prices unduly as long as the Fed demonstrates its commitment to low inflation. In effect, the Fed and the public together sustain a reputational low inflationary equilibrium.

Experience shows that the guiding principle for monetary policy is to preempt rising inflation. The experience with go-stop policy teaches that to wait until the public acknowledges rising inflation to be a problem is to wait too long. By then, higher inflation has become entrenched and must be counteracted by corrective policy actions, which are more likely to depress economic activity.

Even the United States' relatively brief experience with low inflation contains useful insights. In some years, such as 1994, inflationary pressures might be judged to call for a particularly aggressive preemptive tightening. The Fed raised real short-term interest rates by 3 percentage points from February 1994 to February 1995. This action was taken because real economic indicators suggested a reasonable likelihood that inflation would begin to rise in the absence of policy tightening. The real short-term interest rate was near zero prior to the tightening—a level clearly incompatible with price stability. In the event, the Fed's policy actions succeeded in preempting a rise in inflation without sending the economy into recession. From early 1995 to mid-1999, the 30-year bond rate came down from 8 percent to around 5.5 percent; real GDP grew by 2, 2.8, 3.8, and 4.2 percent in the years since 1994; the unemployment rate fell from around 6 percent to just over 4 percent; and inflation as measured by the consumer price index fell by about a percentage point to around 2 percent a year. Clearly, monetary policy does not deserve all the credit for this remarkable outcome; favorable real factors are responsible for much if not most of the extraordinary results. The experience shows, however, that a well-timed preemptive monetary policy tightening is nothing to be feared. In fact, the Fed's tightening in 1994 was almost certainly necessary to keep inflation from destabilizing the economy and ending the business expansion, as it had done many times before in U.S. history.

The Fed appears to have acquired some additional credibility for low inflation because of the 1994 policy tightening. It was able to lower short-term rates by three-quarters of a percentage point in the fall of 1998, to stabilize the world financial system in the wake of the Russian default, yet there has so far been no hint of an inflation scare as a result of this easing. A key to effective management of monetary policy over the business cycle is to move short-term interest rates up decisively and preemptively when warranted, to build credibility for low inflation. With credibility "in the bank," so to speak, the Fed can then hold rates steady or move them down out of concern for financial instability or unemployment at other times. The lesson is that credibility enhances flexibility.

Conclusion

The recommended priority for price stability derives from the evidence just summarized, which shows that credibility for low inflation is the cornerstone of effective monetary policy. A formal inflation target, with or without a legislative mandate, helps lock in that credibility. It is important to stress, however, that an inflation target does not preclude a central bank from taking actions to stabilize employment and financial markets in the short run. As mentioned above, an inflation target enhances flexibility by increasing credibility. Ultimately a central bank can only secure full credibility for low inflation with the backing and understanding of the government and the public. A legislatively mandated inflation target helps deepen the public's understanding and support by creating a document that can be studied and explained in the nation's schools and discussed more fully in the press. Stabilization of the price level then passes from the domain of politics to become one of the institutional foundations of the economy.

Reference

Romer, Christina, and David Romer, 1989, "Does Monetary Policy Matter? A Test in the Spirit of Friedman and Schwartz," *NBER Macroeconomics Annual*, Vol. 4, pp. 121–70.

3 # Strategic Choices in Inflation Targeting: The New Zealand Experience

Murray Sherwin

The Reserve Bank of New Zealand Act of 1989, which established the independence of the Reserve Bank of New Zealand (RBNZ, New Zealand's central bank) and set the single objective of price stability for the country's monetary policy, came into force in 1990. The first Policy Targets Agreement (PTA) specifically defining the inflation target was signed in March of that year. However, in New Zealand the adoption of the concept and practice of inflation targeting, in the sense of an announced, numerical target, is dated from April 1988. Indeed, several years before that, in the middle of 1984, the government had made it clear that the achievement of low inflation was a key objective of its economic policy agenda.

In an operational sense, New Zealand's approach to monetary policy in the mid-1980s was encapsulated in two key initiatives. The first was the decision in March 1985 to move to a clean float of the New Zealand dollar. That has been sustained ever since, with no direct foreign exchange market intervention by the RBNZ over the subsequent 14 years. The second key decision was to adopt the principle that all of the government's funding requirements should be met in private markets, primarily through open tenders. With those two decisions, the major exogenous influences on the money base were removed. Those decisions also signaled the government's willingness to accept the markets' judgment with respect to the behavior of interest rates and the exchange rate, at least within very wide ranges.

Inflation Targeting in Concept

There is a tendency in some quarters to see inflation targeting as a complex solution, with the complexities arising from the perceived need for:

- a well-developed forecasting technology;

- certain specific forms of institutional structure, often including central bank independence;

- a sound and well-developed financial sector; and

- well-developed measures of inflation.

In fact, New Zealand scored rather poorly on each of those characteristics when the serious attack on inflation was first launched. Forecasting systems were not particularly sophisticated, as the existing econometric models had essentially been rendered redundant by the extensive structural reform then under way in New Zealand. The RBNZ Act was not passed until about five years after the country had embarked on the disinflationary process. New Zealand's financial sector in the second half of the 1980s was far from sound and stable, with one significant collapse and a couple of near misses. And inflation measures were far from ideal—and in some respects they remain so.

The essence of inflation targeting seems to boil down to the following:

- Decide what level of inflation is appropriate to the economy.

- Ensure that there is political acceptance of that objective, however defined.

- Set monetary policy with the intention of meeting that inflation target and keeping inflation low thereafter.

The rest is essentially of second-order importance, albeit with plenty of scope for complication and distraction.

The New Zealand Context

The comprehensiveness of New Zealand's policy reforms over the period since 1984 provides an important backdrop to any assessment of the effectiveness of the inflation targeting regime. Inflation targeting was not introduced in isolation. Rather, it was introduced in the midst of a process that involved substantial industry deregulation (including that of the financial sector); privatization and corporatization within the state enterprise sector; tariff and border protection reforms; sweeping tax reforms; labor market reforms; removal of industry subsidies; the complete removal of all capital controls and the subsequent free float of the exchange rate; and rigorous and comprehensive fiscal reform.[1]

---

[1]See Brash (1996) for a review of the New Zealand reform process.

Many of these reforms contributed to the process of breaking down "institutionalized" inflation, as embodied in the indexation of wages and prices, a "cost plus" pricing mentality, and a crawling peg for the exchange rate. However, some reforms conspired to slow the disinflation process, such as the introduction of a goods and services tax (GST; a comprehensive consumption tax in the style of a value-added tax) and the move to "user pays" principles for many government-provided services.

Much of the public sector reform process in New Zealand drew heavily on the principal-agent model. As applied to most government agencies, this model required that the principal (that is, the government, as represented by the relevant cabinet minister) and the agent (the chief executive of the government department in question) enter into a contract specifying the "outputs" to be produced and the nature of the department's accountabilities to the minister. The origins of inflation targeting in New Zealand flowed more or less directly from the application of that model to the central bank.

The New Zealand Framework

The key features of the New Zealand framework are as follows: [2]

- A single objective for monetary policy, price stability, is enshrined in law.

- The RBNZ has effective independence to implement monetary policy as it judges necessary to meet its contracted target, without limitations on the techniques it may use, except that its choices "must have regard to the efficiency and soundness of the financial system."

- The legislation recognizes that any choices on the trade-offs between monetary policy and other economic policy objectives are the prerogative of the elected government.

- The way in which such trade-offs are made is a matter of public record and therefore transparent to the community at large.

- Operational independence is accompanied by clear accountability for all decisions on monetary policy implementation. The governor of the RBNZ is solely responsible for monetary policy outcomes in terms of the target to which he or she agreed when accepting the position.

A committee of nonexecutive directors of the RBNZ's governing board exists whose principal function is to monitor the governor's performance in

---

[2]This section draws heavily on Nicholl and Archer (1992).

terms of the PTA. The committee has no involvement in monetary policy decisions but is required to review those decisions and to report its views periodically to the national treasurer. The committee may recommend the dismissal of the governor should it conclude that he or she is not diligently striving to meet the target assigned in the PTA.

The Framework in Practice

The institutional framework just described has been in place now for a decade, but it has evolved considerably over those years. In part, the new developments have reflected shifting circumstances: the task of maintaining price stability is different, and in some senses more difficult, than the task of disinflating. In part, there have been shifts in the RBNZ's thinking about key issues: in particular, its views on the relative roles of interest rates and exchange rates in monetary policy transmission have shifted. Also, the implementation structure has proved less than satisfactory at times and has been subject to change. As the implementation of inflation targeting has progressed, public acceptance of the price stability target has grown, and with that acceptance, inflation expectations appear to have become better anchored. That has allowed some latitude in policy implementation that was not available early in the process.

The international environment has changed as well: inflation pressures from abroad are not what they were a decade ago. That has an impact both on local inflation expectations and on the other external pressures that New Zealand faces. Finally, the RBNZ has learned from experience and from mistakes. No doubt, it will continue to learn from both.

The 1990 Model

As already noted, the first PTA under the RBNZ Act was signed in March 1990. At the time, the consumer price index (CPI) was running at a little over 5 percent a year (Figure 1), and the economy was in recession. The PTA formally confirmed a target of 0–2 percent for the CPI, to be achieved by the year ending December 1992. That original PTA also established a number of "caveats" or exceptions to the target. These were interpreted as providing a capacity to look through the direct impact on the CPI arising from interest rate changes, significant movements in public sector charges, shifts in the GST and local government taxes, or significant movements in export or import prices.

In practice, these caveats were implemented through the preparation of a measure of underlying inflation that was "PTA consistent." In other words, the underlying inflation measure was derived from the headline CPI measure cal-

Figure 1
New Zealand: Inflation as Measured by the Consumer Price Index, and Underlying Inflation
(In percent per year)

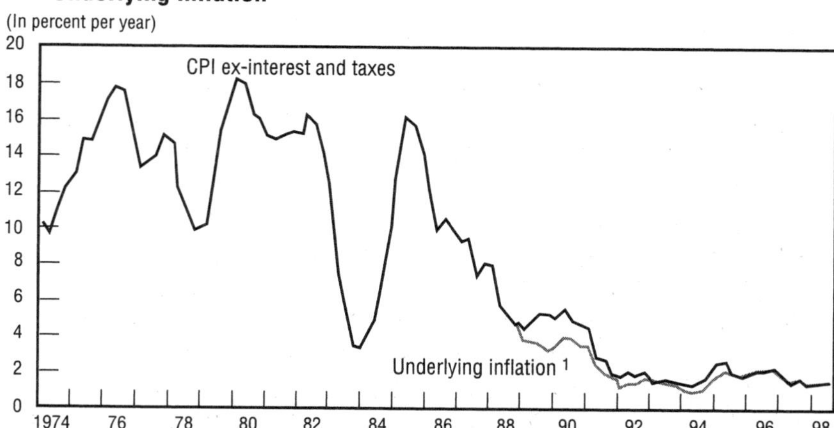

Source: Statistics New Zealand and Reserve Bank of New Zealand data.
[1] Underlying inflation is derived from the Statistics New Zealand CPI–All Groups series, adjusted by excluding the impact of interest rates, taxes, and other significant price shocks as provided for in the RBNZ policy targets agreement at the time.

culated by the government statisticians, but adjusted to take account of the exceptions listed above. This underlying inflation measure became the operational target.

Although the PTA does not require it, the RBNZ opted to publish an indicative trajectory for inflation, bridging the gap between the starting point of over 5 percent and the targeted rate of less than 2 percent. Accordingly, targets of 3–5 percent were set for 1990 and 1.5–3.5 percent for 1991. A change in government in the second half of 1990 led to an amended PTA being signed, which deferred the 0–2 percent target by one year.

During the initial phases of formal inflation targeting, the RBNZ tended to emphasize the importance of not breaching the target. In its public discussion of policy and in its policy reactions, the central bank tended to treat the inflation target as "hard-edged." Indeed, the target was sometimes described as being bounded by electric fences: approach if you must, but do not touch! The hard edges were not necessarily a conscious part of the original design of the framework. Rather, they emerged once inflation had fallen to within the target range. They came to prominence in the context of an extensive public communications program aimed at convincing New Zealanders that the central bank was indeed serious about its inflation target and intended to adhere to it over the long haul.

The RBNZ has a long history of publishing its forecasts. Continuation of that policy seemed natural in the context of the new regime with its emphasis on transparency and accountability. The new regime brought an additional publication requirement in the form of twice-yearly Monetary Policy Statements. Since forecasts were already being published every six months, this allowed the RBNZ to move to alternating quarterly publication of projections and statements. The early statements tended to concentrate on explaining and interpreting the new framework and describing the RBNZ's policy reaction function: what indicators it was watching and how it might respond to movements in those indicators.

The 1999 Model

The PTA in effect as of this writing (May 1999) was signed in December 1997 and sets the inflation target in terms of the All Groups Consumers Price Index excluding Credit Services (CPIX), as published by Statistics New Zealand. The target is 12-monthly increases in the CPIX between zero and 3 percent. The PTA recognizes that significant temporary shocks can occur that mask the underlying trend in prices. The RBNZ is instructed to respond to such disturbances in a manner that prevents general inflationary pressures from emerging.

The PTA explicitly notes that there will be occasions when inflation outcomes deviate from the targeted range. On those occasions it requires the RBNZ to explain in its Monetary Policy Statements why such outcomes have occurred and the nature of its monetary policy response.

The edges of the target band have been softened compared with those in the original PTA. The RBNZ has moved away from any formal accounting of the various caveats embodied in its earlier underlying inflation measure. Instead, it has adopted a process of describing and accounting for, ex post, any shocks or exogenous influences on inflation and explaining how the central bank views these for the purposes of formulating policy.

In practice, as already noted, the monetary policy process revolves around a quarterly cycle centered on the production of comprehensive economic projections and their subsequent publication in the RBNZ's quarterly statements.[3] The projection process identifies, with all the usual constraints, qualifiers, and limitations, the monetary conditions that will be necessary to maintain CPIX inflation at the midpoint of the 0–3 percent target band over the next two to

---

[3]Recent Monetary Policy Statements can be viewed on the RBNZ's World Wide Web site: http://www.rbnz.govt.nz.

three years. On that basis, the RBNZ announces its official cash rate (OCR), the interest rate that is the principal instrument of policy. The OCR is reviewed formally, but without the aid of a fully developed set of projections, approximately midway between each of the quarterly statements, giving eight possible reset points for the OCR each year.

In general, when looking at the stance of policy, the RBNZ is making an assessment about likely domestic price pressures six to eight quarters ahead. Today's policy settings are aimed at delivering an inflation rate in the middle part of the target range in that time frame. However, the RBNZ is also conscious that the starting point is uncertain. Important data series in New Zealand are slow to arrive and may be subject to revision. Thus, as much as one tries to look forward, the RBNZ knows that its attitude to current policy is likely to be heavily conditioned by emerging data on the recent past.

Lessons Learned

Bernanke and others (1999) identify a number of key operational issues that arise in the design and implementation of an inflation targeting regime. With the benefit of a decade of experience, how does the RBNZ think about some of those issues?

Which Measure of Inflation Should Be Used?

New Zealand opted for the price measure already most familiar to New Zealanders, namely, the CPI. The disadvantages of some aspects of the construction of the CPI were recognized, but none of the alternative measures of inflation were regarded as viable candidates.

Over the past couple of years the RBNZ has been working with Statistics New Zealand on a review of the CPI. The officially published measure used for purposes of the inflation target (the CPIX) excludes the interest rate component. In addition, alternative measures of inflation will soon be available that incorporate owner-occupied housing costs by imputing the cost of renting the same house rather than by the current "acquisitions" approach based on home purchase prices and mortgage interest rates.

Some effort has been devoted to exploring trend measures of inflation (Roger, 1995). Although some measures have been identified, such as weighted medians of the CPI components, that have attractive characteristics with respect to trend smoothing, none of these were adopted as the target measure, largely because of the perceived difficulties in gaining public understanding and acceptance. However, the CPIs of many countries carry a higher weighting for volatile elements such as food. In those cases, the identification of a reliable but more stable measure of trend inflation may be much more important for the successful implementation of inflation targeting.

What Numerical Value Should the Target Have?

The original 0–2 percent target in New Zealand reflected a generalized ambition to achieve something close to "true" price stability. At the time, there was a loose presumption that the measurement bias in the CPI could be on the order of 1 percentage point. The shift to a 0–3 percent target in 1996 was essentially politically driven. Donald Brash, the governor of the RBNZ, was not seeking such a change himself, even though inflation had slightly exceeded the 2 percent upper limit through the previous year. But there is reason to believe that the original target suffered to some degree from a public perception that it was too narrow to be fully credible. It is also fair to say that the RBNZ was, and remains, very comfortable with the extra latitude of the new target. The wider band is more consistent with what the central bank believes is achievable with a reasonable degree of reliability. It is also more consistent with a growing sense that a little additional inflation variability can be traded off against some increased stability in output and interest rates. This matter is discussed further below.

What Time Horizon Should Be Set?

The question of the appropriate policy horizon is essentially bound up with the nature of the chosen target and with the arrangements in place to ensure accountability. With a hard-edged target and rigorous accountability for outcomes relative to the target, the incentives facing the central bank lead it toward shorter horizons and more active manipulation of the policy instruments.

The RBNZ's early horizons were around the one-year mark. That was broadly consistent with what the central bank felt its forecasting capacity to be. It was also consistent with the approach to implementation, which at the time put a good deal of emphasis on the direct price effects of exchange rate movements. More recently, more weight has been placed on interest rates and the indirect impact of the exchange rate on prices. It is now assumed, in the first instance and in the absence of evidence to the contrary, that shifts in the exchange rate are real rather than nominal in character and do not require an immediate interest rate response. The direct price consequences are therefore assumed to be transitory and, for that reason, best ignored. In this respect, New Zealand has moved in the direction of the Reserve Bank of Australia.

Consistent with that evolving view of the role of the exchange rate, the policy horizon was lengthened to between six and eight quarters. In doing so, the RBNZ acknowledges that the longer horizon leads directly to a greater risk that it will miss the target range more often. Work has recently been published that looks at these questions directly (Drew and Orr, 1999). The RBNZ's stylized policy simulation work, summarized in Table 1, suggests that, with a band width of plus or minus 1.5 percent, given the RBNZ's standard six- to eight-quarter policy horizon, the probability that inflation outcomes will be within the band is 66 percent under the least active policy rule. This probability rises to 92 percent under the most active policy rule. With all the usual qualifications that should accompany analysis of this sort, one can conclude that:

- The narrower the target range, the more active monetary policy must be.

- More activism implies more variability in interest rates, the exchange rate, and output, and (up to a point) less variability in inflation.

- Lower inflation expectations and a wider target range allow for a longer policy horizon and less active monetary policy.

Should the Target Be Specified as a Point or as a Range?

The issues that arise in deciding between point and range are essentially the same as those in the debates over the width of the band and the policy horizon. By widening and softening the edges of the bands, the RBNZ has moved more in the direction of an Australian-style "thick point." It is felt that this is an option more readily contemplated now, with inflationary expectations becoming better anchored, than it could have been in the very early stages of New Zealand's inflation targeting experience.

Certainly, a disadvantage of the bands approach is the tendency to focus unwarranted attention on very small deviations from the target (2.99 percent inflation equals success, whereas 3.01 percent inflation equals failure). In that sense, the potential credibility gains from hard-edged bands dissipate as time passes and success in achieving and maintaining price stability grows.

Table 1. New Zealand: Probabilities of Successful Targeting Under Different Band Widths and Policy Reactions

Band width (percentage points)	Probability that inflation will lie within the band after six to eight quarters (percent)			
	Least active policy[1]	Less active policy	More active policy	Most active policy
± 1	50	70	64	75
± 1.5	66	82	90	92
± 2	80	93	97	98
± 3	95	99	99	99

Source: Drew and Orr (1999).

[1]The policy reaction is made more active by increasing the size of the interest rate response to a deviation from the inflation target.

Transparency

Transparency is an integral part of the RBNZ's framework. The explicit and transparent commitment to price stability has undoubtedly brought focus to the task of monetary policy. The target is clear and has a high public profile. The RBNZ cannot escape difficult monetary policy decisions—indeed, it is obliged to confront them early.

Within political circles, the clarity and transparency of the framework appear to have modified the nature of the monetary policy debate. The proposition that New Zealand should aim for price stability, or some close approximation, has proved difficult to challenge politically. Instead, the political debate has tended to center around particular aspects of the framework—such as the specification of the target (for example, the appropriate band width and midpoint), or the different sectoral impacts of monetary policy—rather than on the desirability of maintaining a firm commitment to price stability.

For the public at large, the target is highly visible and readily monitored. The RBNZ has a comprehensive public information and outreach program that attempts to explain what monetary policy is about and why. The program encompasses the production of pamphlets, resource material for schools, speeches, articles, interviews, and a very active Internet site. The aims of the program lie primarily in influencing inflationary expectations, strengthening the credibility of the target, and through that, increasing the likelihood that the central bank will both achieve its target and minimize any social costs in doing so.

Accountability

As noted at the outset, the New Zealand framework grew out of the general application of the principal-agent model throughout the public sector. Clear specification of objectives and accountabilities is integral to that model. The New Zealand inflation targeting model apparently goes further than others in specifying the potential consequences for nonperformance under the target. That seems to be a helpful provision, as it reinforces the institutional incentives toward the achievement of price stability and, probably, the public's willingness to believe that the inflation target will be met.

An unusual aspect of the New Zealand framework is its assignment of decision-making authority and responsibility solely in the person of the governor. The purpose of that was made quite clear. It was intended to eliminate any ambiguity about where responsibility for the conduct of monetary policy rests, and in that way to sharpen the incentives for delivery of price stability. There seems little doubt that it has had that effect.

Implementation Structures

New Zealand's monetary policy implementation structures have proved less than satisfactory on occasion. In the early stages of the formal targeting regime, the RBNZ relied heavily on the direct price effects from changes in the exchange rate, using a form of variable exchange rate comfort zones. At times this was supplemented by references to the slope of the yield curve, and more recently target zones for a monetary conditions index have been announced. All of these arrangements were products of a historical attachment to a quantity-based implementation structure. The monetary policy instrument at the base of each was the quantity of "settlement cash" made available to the banking system.

Over the years, it became apparent that the relationship between the quantity of settlement cash made available to the banking system and prevailing monetary conditions was very elastic. For that reason, the settlement cash target ceased to be an effective policy instrument or a reliable policy signal. It was also apparent that the implementation structure being employed was encouraging an unhelpful degree of volatility in short-term interest rates and, in doing so, complicating the task of communicating the RBNZ's desired policy stance. Accordingly, in March 1999 the quantity-based implementation structure was abandoned in favor of a fairly conventional structure built around fixing the overnight interbank cash rate.

These arrangements are not central to the issue of inflation targeting, but it is worth noting in passing that there are important considerations embodied in the choice of an implementation structure, which can ease or complicate the conduct of monetary policy. The risk of a poorly specified implementation structure is that it will distract from the longer-term objectives of policy.

Assessing the New Zealand Experience

Inflation outcomes were consistent with the assigned target from 1991 to mid-1995, although some overshooting occurred through 1995 and 1996 before the target was adjusted. Perhaps a more relevant measure of success is New Zealand's inflation performance relative to that in other countries (Figure 2). On that basis, one can see that New Zealand has moved from being one of the worst performers among the industrial countries with respect to inflation to somewhere clearly in the middle of the pack. In terms of the objectives set for monetary policy under the 1989 act, that can only be described as a successful performance.

Judging how much of that improved performance can be ascribed to the particular inflation targeting regime that was adopted is a much harder task. One could assign great importance to the shifts in political priorities, to the

Figure 2
Inflation in New Zealand and Other Industrial Countries

(In percent per year)

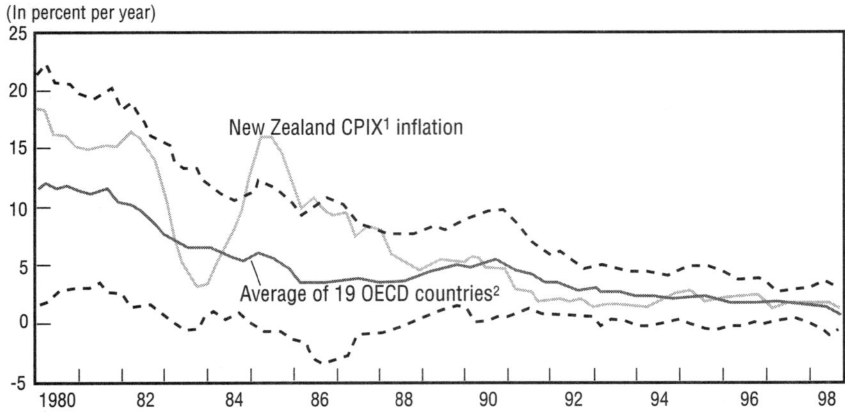

Source: Brooke, Collins, and Smith (1998).
[1] All Groups Consumer Price Index Excluding Credit Services.
[2] Dashed lines represent 2 standard deviations above and below the average.

sweeping reforms that have occurred elsewhere in New Zealand's macroeconomic and microeconomic policies, and to the shift in trading partners' inflationary behavior. It could be argued, for instance, that the shift in political attitudes toward inflation was, ultimately, the only change that really mattered. One could also reasonably argue that the key changes came with the decisions to float the exchange rate and to commit to market financing of the government's fiscal deficits.

To accept those arguments, however, would miss some important points. Certainly, the political will to adopt a price stability target was an essential prerequisite to any serious attack on institutionalized inflation. However, the inflation targeting regime has given that initial political commitment a degree of durability that transcends the influence of the particular set of politicians in power in 1989, when the RBNZ Act became law. Incentives were shifted from an acceptance of inflation arising from the usual time-inconsistent influences toward a more robust resistance to any future reemergence of inflationary tendencies.

References

Bernanke, Ben, Thomas Laubach, Frederic Mishkin, and Adam Posen, 1999, *Inflation Targeting: Lessons from the International Experience* (Princeton, New Jersey: Princeton University Press).

Brash, Donald T., 1996, "New Zealand's Remarkable Reforms," Fifth Annual Hayek Memorial Lecture (London: Institute of Economic Affairs).

Drew, Aaron, and Adrian Orr, 1999, "The Reserve Bank's Role in the Recent Business Cycle: Actions and Evolution," *Reserve Bank of New Zealand Bulletin,* Vol. 62, No. 1, pp. 5–24.

Nicholl, Peter, and David Archer, 1992, "An Announced Downward Path for Inflation," *Reserve Bank of New Zealand Bulletin,* Vol. 5, No. 4, pp. 315–23.

Roger, Scott, 1995, "Measures of Underlying Inflation in New Zealand, 1981–95," Reserve Bank of New Zealand Discussion Paper Series No. G95/5.

4 Inflation Forecast Targeting: The Swedish Experience

Claes Berg[1]

An inflation target can serve as a nominal anchor, aiming at coordinating inflation expectations. As a nominal anchor, an inflation target also provides a commitment mechanism that increases the accountability of the monetary policy authority. The inflation target communicates to the public the inflation rate at which the central bank will aim in the future. It thus serves as a reference point against which the central bank can be judged.

In January 1993 the Sveriges Riksbank, the central bank of Sweden, specified that the objective of monetary policy would henceforth be to limit the annual increase in the headline consumer price index (CPI) in 1995 and beyond to 2 percent, with a tolerance of plus or minus 1 percentage point. This objective corresponded to the so-called underlying rate of inflation when the target was announced. In 1993 and in 1994 as well, monetary policy aimed at preventing the inflationary impulse (which was deemed unavoidable) due to a large depreciation of the krona and changes in indirect taxes from causing a persistent increase in the underlying rate of inflation. The experience of the first years of inflation targeting in connection with the most recent amendments to the 1988 Riksbank Act, which came into force on January 1, 1999, and prescribe an explicit objective for monetary policy, gave reasons to clarify the formulation of monetary policy.

Maintaining Price Stability

The principles on which monetary policy decisions in Sweden are based can be formulated as a simple rule of thumb.[2] If the inflation forecast, based on an

---

[1] The views expressed here are solely the responsibility of the author and should not be interpreted as reflecting the views of the Executive Board of Sveriges Riksbank.

[2] For a more technical presentation see Svensson (1999).

unchanged rate of interest on repurchase agreements (repos), is in line with the target at the appropriate time horizon, the monetary stance is appropriate. If the forecast is above (below) the inflation target, the monetary stance is too expansionary (restrictive), and the repo rate should be raised (lowered) immediately or in the near future. As this rule of thumb refers to an inflation forecast that assumes the instrumental rate (the repo rate) is unchanged, it is natural for the Riksbank to present its forecasts accordingly.

Dealing with Forecast Uncertainty

Each forecasting round at the Riksbank culminates in a main scenario that is described in its quarterly *Inflation Report*.[3] It should be stressed that the main scenario is viewed as the most likely outcome under the assumption that the repo rate is held constant over the forecast horizon. The assumption of an unchanged repo rate is made primarily for presentational reasons, to show whether or not the repo rate needs to be changed to bring inflation in line with the target.

The statistical measure that best corresponds to the forecast in the main scenario is the mode (Figure 1), since it is the most likely outcome in the distribution (or rather, the value that corresponds to the maximum of the density function). However, monetary policy is not guided by the most likely outcome only. An assessment of the risk spectrum is also important, and in practice the mean forecast of future inflation is therefore taken into consideration when deciding on the appropriate monetary policy stance.[4] In recent inflation reports, confidence intervals for the forecasts have been published. The executive board of the Riksbank may take the properties of the whole distribution into account when setting the repo rate. This implies that monetary policy can be described as being guided by "distribution forecast" targeting.[5]

Uncertainty analysis is based on two types of assessments for each factor that is deemed to affect inflation. First, an assessment is made as to whether or not the uncertainty in the forecast related to each factor is greater or less than

---

[3]This section is based on Blix and Sellin (1998). See, for example, the *Inflation Report* for the fourth quarter of 1998 for a discussion of the framework for the forecast.

[4]Focusing on the mean forecast also facilitates the use of econometric models, which normally produce forecasts of the mean.

[5]Svensson (1999) shows that nonlinearity and uncertainty about the model both imply that certainty-equivalence does not apply. This means it is not optimal to use conditional mean forecasts as intermediate variables. Therefore he suggests that conditional probability distributions of the target variables be used rather than only the means. In practice, this form of distribution targeting is implemented in an elementary way, as the Riksbank staff construct paths for inflation and the output gap, given various interest rate paths, which are presented to the executive board.

Figure 1
Skewed Forecast Distribution

Mode (main scenario)

Median

Mean

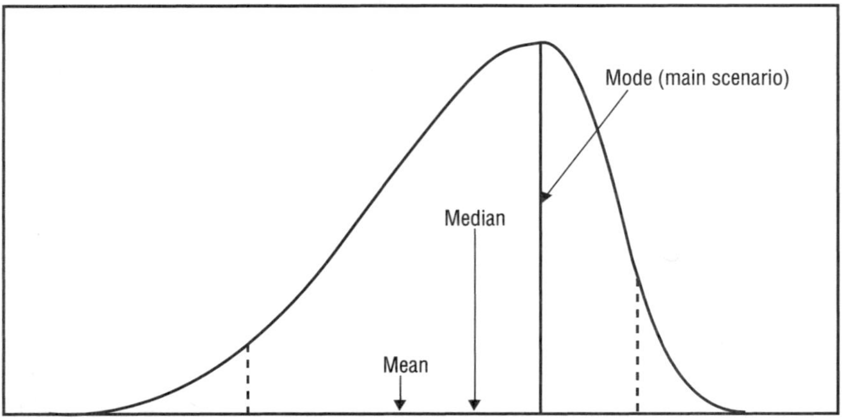

Note: Dashed lines represent 90 percent confidence interval.

that historically associated with the factor in question. Second, an assessment is made as to whether the probability of outcomes above the main scenario exceeds the probability of outcomes below (that is, whether the distribution of outcomes is normal). The resulting distributions are then weighed together to arrive at an inflation-asymmetric estimate of risk. For each factor these assessments are then summarized in a two-part forecast distribution, with weights that reflect each factor's relative importance for future inflation.

The inflation forecasts from the main scenario that are published in the *Inflation Report* (since the second quarter of 1998) are presented with uncertainty bands derived using the inflation forecast distributions just described (Figure 2). The bands are constructed such that the probability of outcomes below the lower band equals that of outcomes above the upper band.

Dealing with Transitory Effects

Since the inflation target came into force at the beginning of 1995, the annual increase in consumer prices has averaged 1.1 percent. This average outcome is below the targeted figure but within the tolerance interval. Over the same period, the average underlying rate of inflation has been somewhat higher: 1.7 percent in terms of the UND1X (the CPI excluding interest expenditure and the direct effects of indirect taxes and subsidies) and 2.3 percent in terms of the UNDINHX (which, in addition, excludes goods that are mainly imported; Figure 3). This shows that, during these four years, transitory effects on inflation have been stronger overall on the downside than on the upside.

Figure 2

Sweden: Inflation as Measured by the CPI and Inflation Projections

(In percent per year)[1]

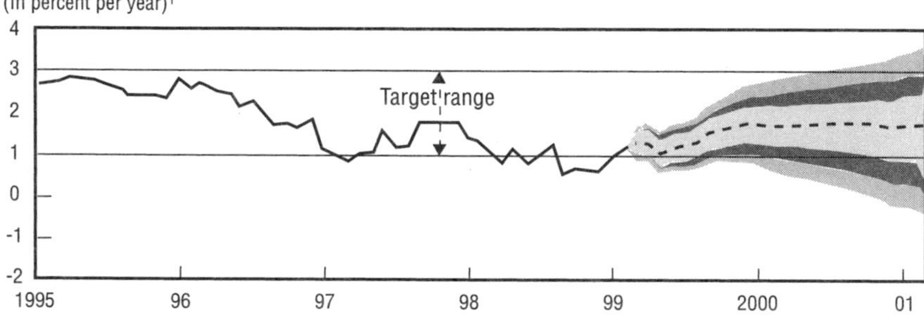

Source: Statistics Sweden and Sveriges Riksbank, *Inflation Report,* March 1999.
[1] Change in the CPI over the previous 12 months. Shaded areas represent 50, 75, and 90 percent confidence intervals.

Figure 3

Sweden: CPI Inflation and Two Alternative Measures of Inflation

(In percent per year)[1]

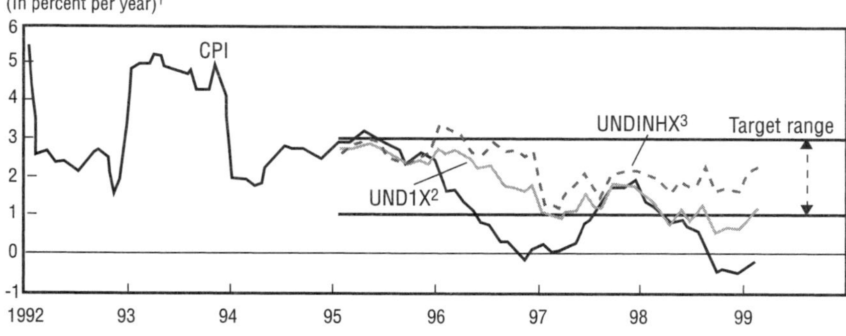

Source: Statistics Sweden.
[1] Change in the index over the previous 12 months.
[2] CPI excluding interest expenditure and direct effects of indirect taxes and subsidies.
[3] CPI excluding interest expenditure, goods that are mainly imported, and direct effects of domestic indirect taxes and subsidies.

When the Swedish inflation target was clarified in 1999, it was modified in two respects. The first concerns situations when CPI inflation in the relevant time horizon is being affected by specific factors that are judged to have no substantial permanent impact on inflation or the inflation process. For example, a repo rate adjustment, up or down, affects house mortgage interest expenditure, which is a sizable component of the CPI, but clearly this is not an effect on the CPI that the Riksbank ought to counter. Monetary policy effects of indirect taxes and subsidies can be analyzed in a similar way. When policy is formulated in these situations, there may be grounds for explaining *in advance* that a deviation from the CPI target is warranted.

The Target Horizon

The second modification in the formulation of the inflation target relates to circumstances in which inflation for some reason has deviated markedly from the target.[6] Experience in Sweden as well as studies across countries suggest that the lag before monetary policy elicits its main effect is one to two years. This horizon for the main effect of monetary policy implies that policy should be guided by inflation forecasts five to eight quarters ahead. The target horizon, however, is not necessarily the same as the horizon for the main effect of monetary policy. Normally it is, but in the event of a sizable deviation from the target, there are always grounds for weighing the benefits of a rapid return to the target against the consequences for the real economy.[7]

Accountability

The amendments to the Riksbank Act that came into force on January 1, 1999, were designed to give the Swedish central bank greater independence from political influence, establish a primary objective for monetary policy (namely, price stability), and ensure the Riksbank's accountability for achievement of its policy objective.[8]

Because monetary policy cannot control future inflation with absolute precision, inflation will fluctuate around the targeted rate. There are several grounds for setting a tolerance interval for these fluctuations. One is that it may be useful in the assessment of monetary policy by the body to which the central bank is accountable.

Two recent measures aim at clarifying the role of the tolerance band. First, after the new central bank legislation went into force, the assessment of monetary policy by the Riksdag (the national legislature) was clarified. In this context, the tolerance interval will have an operational function. The Riksbank has announced that whenever CPI inflation is outside the tolerance interval, it will

---

[6]For references, see Bernanke and Gertler (1995) and Gerlach and Smets (1994).

[7]See Heikensten and Vredin (1998) for a discussion of flexible inflation targeting.

[8]With regard to exchange rate policy, the government will have the authority to decide, after consultation with the Riksbank, on the choice of exchange rate regime. The Riksbank will have responsibility for implementing the exchange rate regime adopted by the government. This means, for example, that the Riksbank will decide on the central rate and the band width in a fixed exchange rate system and on the practical application of policies in a floating rate system. The first step toward making the Riksbank more independent was taken already in 1988. For a discussion of the Swedish debate, see Heikensten and Vredin (1998).

present an explanation for why this has occurred. This clarification, suggested by Heikensten and Vredin (1998), was inspired by the rule requiring the Bank of England, as soon as inflation strays outside a specified interval, to write an open letter explaining why inflation is not on target. Second, to highlight the statistical uncertainties in the inflation forecasts, since mid-1998 the *Inflation Report* has included a table showing the probabilities of inflation falling within the tolerance interval 12 and 24 months out, assuming an unchanged stance of monetary policy.

Evaluation of monetary policy decisions requires knowledge of the analysis and discussion that preceded them. One way to facilitate effective monitoring of the central bank is to publish the minutes of the decision-making body. The executive board of the Riksbank has decided to hold monetary policy meetings 8 to 10 times a year, and the minutes are published with a lag of two to four weeks.

Implementation of Monetary Policy in Sweden Since 1993

The implementation and communication of monetary policy since 1993 can be divided into three phases. In the first phase, 1993–95, the inflation targeting strategy was announced and established. During the first two years of this period, the objective was to prevent the underlying rate of inflation from increasing. Regular (thrice-yearly) publication of a report on inflation and inflation expectations in Sweden began during this period. During this phase, bond investors' long-term (five years) inflation expectations fell from above 4 percent to 3 percent, that is, to the upper bound of the tolerance interval. During this period, however, the Riksbank did not publish inflation forecasts. The risks for future inflation were stated in the reports in a more general way.

In the second phase, 1996–97, inflation forecast targeting was introduced. The Riksbank's own inflation forecasts were given more weight in the communication of monetary policy. Forecasts of future inflation were gradually introduced in the reports, whose name was changed to *Inflation Report*. During this phase, bond investors' five-year inflation expectations fell from 3 percent to around 2½ percent by the end of 1997 (Figure 4), implying that the inflation target was gaining credibility.

In the third phase, from 1998 onward, "distribution forecast targeting" was introduced, and explicit paths for future inflation were published, surrounded by confidence intervals. Long-term inflation expectations during this period were slightly below 2 percent (Table 1), signaling the credibility of the inflation targeting strategy.

Figure 4
Sweden: Repo Rate and Long-Term Inflation Expectations
(In percent per year)

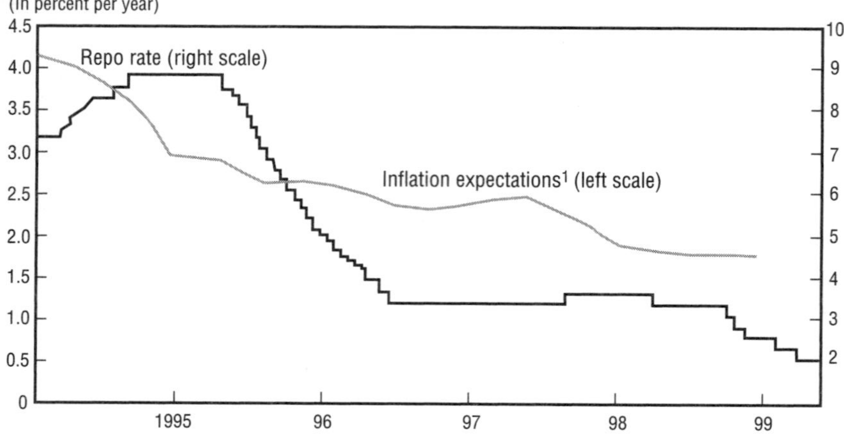

Source: Aragon Fondkommission and Sveriges Riksbank.
[1] Expectations are for the inflation rate five years hence as reported by the Aragon Survey.

Impact on the Economy

Economic growth in recent years has been in line with that in the rest of the world, after a long period of slower average growth in Sweden. Inflation in Sweden since 1992 has been low and accompanied by declining inflation ex-

Table 1. Sweden: Inflation Forecasts and Associated Uncertainty

	Date of forecast			
	June 1998	September 1998	December 1998	March 1999
End of forecast horizon	June 2000	September 2000	December 2000	March 2000
Forecast of 12-month CPI inflation[1] (percent a year)	1.6	1.9	1.4	1.4
Forecast of 12-month underlying inflation[1,2] (percent a year)	1.8	2.0	1.8	1.8
Uncertainty in the inflation assessment	Normal	Above normal	Slightly above normal	Slightly above normal
Risk assessment	Downside risks dominate	Symmetric	Downside risks dominate	Downside risks dominate

Source: Sveriges Riksbank.
[1]At the end of the forecast horizon.
[2]UND1 (calculated by the Sveriges Riksbank) in June and September 1998; UND1X in December 1998 and March 1999 (calculated by Statistics Sweden).

Figure 5
Sweden: CPI and Inflation Expectations of Households

(In percent per year)

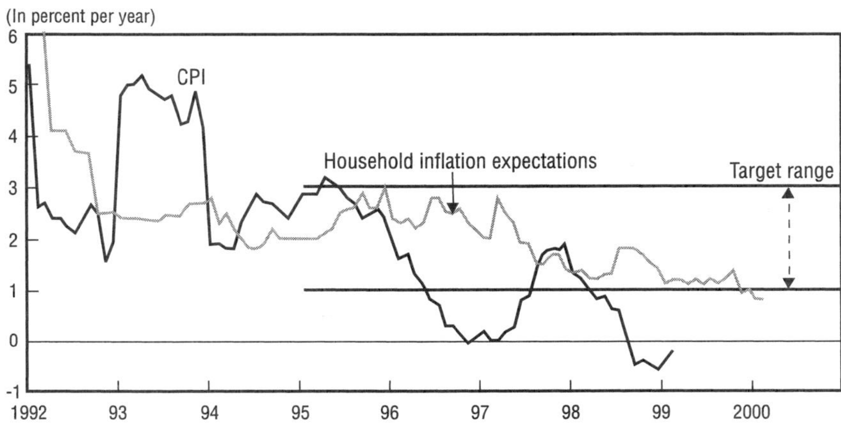

Source: Statistics Sweden and National Institute of Economic Research.
[1] Change in the CPI over the previous 12 months.

pectations and rising credibility of monetary policy. The sharp fall in households' inflation expectations is itself a clear sign of increased credibility for the inflation target. Whereas in the 1980s inflation expectations for the coming 12 months averaged 6.5 percent, since the beginning of 1992 they have averaged slightly below 2 percent. The clear break in households' inflation expectations in 1992 (Figure 5) can be interpreted as an initial sign of a downward shift in the inflation process.

The Riksbank´s view on the exchange rate has altered in some respects since 1992. Gradually more emphasis has been placed on the krona´s forecast path, and occasional fluctuations have been played down. A simple analysis shows that the confidence of market agents in Swedish economic policy, measured as the difference between Swedish and German long-term interest rates, can explain almost a third of Sweden's nominal exchange rate variability since 1992 (Figure 6). In the period from 1994 to 1996, the swings in credibility, measured in this way, explain almost two-thirds of the movement in the exchange rate.

In the period since 1996, the exchange rate has been comparatively stable except during the widespread turbulence in connection with the international financial crisis in the autumn of 1998. However, even with relatively strong government finances and low inflation, a flexible exchange rate does seem to entail exchange rate fluctuations that are greater than was expected when the krona fell in the autumn of 1992. This experience is shared with other countries that use inflation targeting and may not be related to credibility problems

Figure 6

Sweden: Interest Rate Differential with Germany and Krona–Deutsche Mark Exchange Rate

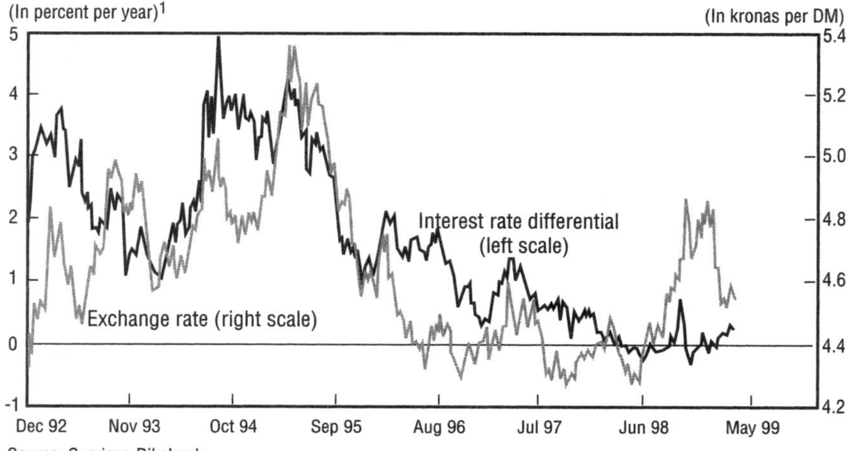

Source: Sveriges Riksbank.
[1] Difference in interest rates on 10–year maturities.

regarding economic policy in Sweden, as is evident from bond market developments. Although the long-term interest rate differential with Germany increased somewhat during the financial turmoil in 1998, it stayed quite small (below 1 percentage point) compared with its levels at the beginning of the floating exchange rate regime.

References

Bernanke, Ben, and Mark Gertler, 1995, "Inside the Black Box: The Credit Channel of Monetary Policy Transmission," *Journal of Economic Perspectives,* Vol. 9 (Fall), pp. 27–48.

Blix, Mårten, and Peter Sellin, 1998, "Uncertainty Bands for Inflation Forecasts," Sveriges Riksbank Working Paper Series No. 65 (Stockholm).

Gerlach, Stefan, and Frank Smets, 1994, "The Monetary Transmission Mechanism: Evidence from the G–7 Countries" (unpublished; Basel: Bank for International Settlements).

Heikensten, Lars, and Anders Vredin, 1998, "Inflation Targeting and Swedish Monetary Policy: Experience and Problems," *Quarterly Review,* Sveriges Riksbank, Vol. 4, pp. 5–33.

Svensson, Lars E.O., 1999, "Price Stability as a Target for Monetary Policy: Defining and Maintaining Price Stability," Sveriges Riksbank Working Paper Series No. 91 (Stockholm).

5

The Canadian Monetary Transmission Mechanism and Inflation Projections

David Longworth[1]

Implementing an inflation targeting regime requires a clear understanding of the monetary policy transmission mechanism and methods of projecting inflation that are consistent with that understanding. This chapter deals with these two aspects of inflation targeting as they apply to the Canadian economy and the Bank of Canada's monetary policy.

The Monetary Policy Transmission Mechanism

The monetary policy transmission mechanism is complex and our understanding of it imperfect. The Bank of Canada's mainstream paradigm is quite explicit and well known and consists of three major sets of linkages. The first is from the instrument, the target band for the overnight (or one-day) interest rate,[2] to other financial variables: the term structure of market interest rates, rates on deposits and loans at financial institutions, and the exchange rate. The second linkage runs from these financial variables to aggregate demand and the output gap. The third set of linkages runs from the output gap, inflation expectations, and the exchange rate to inflation.

The Bank of Canada considers it important to bear in mind that the success and credibility of the monetary and fiscal policy frameworks will condition the way in which the transmission mechanism works in practice. The Bank of Canada also finds it useful to have a checklist of the exogenous shocks that typically hit the economy (bottom of Figure 1).

---

[1]The views expressed in this chapter are those of the author. No responsibility for them should be attributed to the Bank of Canada.

[2]The target band for the overnight interest rate is 50 basis points wide; the Bank of Canada aims to keep the rate in the middle of the band.

Figure 1
Canada: Monetary Policy Transmission Mechanism

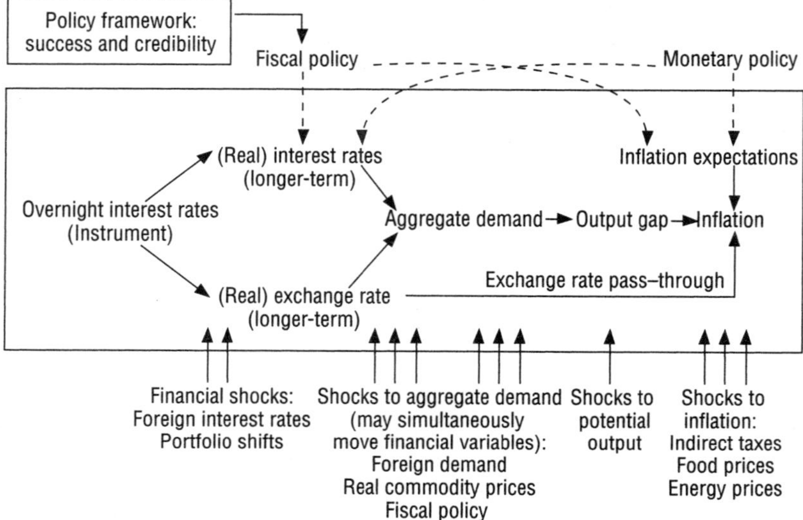

Transmission Through Financial Variables

The term structure of interest rates in Canada is strongly influenced by the term structure of world real interest rates, by risk premiums related to the Canadian government's debt and deficits (relative to those in the rest of the world), and by domestic inflation expectations. However, in the past a rise in nominal domestic short-term rates (and more specifically in recent years, in the target band for the overnight rate) has generally translated into a rise in nominal domestic rates all along the term structure. These effects have typically been smaller, the further out along the maturity spectrum one is looking (Clinton and Zelmer, 1997). Research at the Bank of Canada has concluded that there has been an essentially stable (if not precise) relationship between rates set by deposit-taking financial institutions on loans and deposits and market rates of similar maturities (Clinton and Howard, 1994). The exchange rate responds in an important way to unexpected changes in interest rate differentials between Canada and abroad.

Impact of Financial Variables on Aggregate Demand

As understood at the Bank of Canada, the mainstream transmission mechanism is one in which aggregate demand depends on two variables. The first is real interest rates (relative to equilibrium real interest rates), which affect consumption spending (especially on durable goods) through permanent income effects, and which affect decisions to invest in housing and real business physical capital. The second is the real exchange rate, which affects exports and imports in the usual ways.

The empirical evidence for Canada suggests that short-term (or perhaps short- to medium-term) interest rates matter the most for aggregate demand. The effects of changes in interest rates and the exchange rate on aggregate demand build up only slowly over time. There is little contemporaneous effect, but by the third or the fourth quarter the effect is economically significant, and the maximum effect is reached after six to eight quarters.

Impact on Inflation from the Output Gap, Expectations, and the Exchange Rate

A key part of the Bank of Canada's view of the monetary transmission mechanism is the effect of excess demand or supply in product markets on the rate of inflation. Thus, changes in monetary conditions work through their effect on the output gap to influence the inflation rate over time.

Inflation expectations also play a very important role in the inflation process. Although there is evidence that the backward-looking component in these expectations remains important, the concentration of the central bank on the achievement of its inflation target no doubt helps condition the formation of the forward-looking component.

Other key elements in the short-run inflation process are changes in relative prices. Arising from a number of sources, these can have once-and-for-all effects on the price level and therefore influence the measured inflation rate in the short run, but not necessarily the momentum of the inflation process. Because monetary policy can influence the exchange rate, exchange rate effects are particularly important to note in this regard (see Laflèche, 1996–97). Other specific shocks that have been important in the past include shocks to indirect taxes, energy prices, and food prices.

The Bank of Canada has relied mostly on the output gap channel to influence inflation (including the induced effect of the change in actual inflation thus produced through the backward-looking element of inflation expectations). It did not count on expectations being influenced by the target during the first few years of the inflation targeting regime. Nor has it relied on the exchange rate pass-through to consumer prices to guide inflation to its target. In principle, exploiting the effects of the exchange rate pass-through could shorten the time necessary to hit the inflation target, but at the cost of greater volatility in output.

Inflation Projections

The Bank of Canada uses a Quarterly Projection Model (QPM) as the main model and organizing framework for its medium-term economic projections, which are constructed quarterly. However, both the QPM and other models for inflation alone have been informed by a wide range of research with small models. These models have helped the Bank of Canada reach a better understanding of some of the workings of the economy as well as explore how to impose appropriate theoretical restrictions and grasp their implications.

Longworth and Poloz (1986) constructed a small model to examine various policy rules. Its prominent feature was its simplicity: there were four behavioral equations—for output demand, the inflation-unemployment relationship (a price Phillips curve), money demand, and the exchange rate—plus a policy rule and identities. The framework of the four behavioral equations plus the policy rule captured the mainstream model, in which the real interest rate and the real exchange rate affect the output gap and thus inflation. It also set the stage for subsequent estimation of reduced-form or vector autoregressive (VAR) models, many of which omitted money variables, since the stock of money did not enter the equations for the other variables. For example, Duguay (1994) estimated a reduced-form IS curve for output, in which changes in Canadian output depend on lagged changes in the real interest rate, the real exchange rate, U.S. output, real commodity prices, and a fiscal policy variable. He also presented a short-run Phillips curve.

In the construction of the calibrated QPM, as well as in subsequent work designed to calibrate stochastic shocks for use with the model, a number of VAR models were estimated by Bank of Canada staff. One of the most recent is reported in Black, Macklem, and Rose (1998) and contains six variables: potential output, real commodity prices, the price level, the sum of consumption and investment, the real exchange rate, and the slope of the term structure (the short-term interest rate minus the long-term rate).

Armour and others (1996) have constructed a vector error correction model in which the deviation of money from its long-run demand plays an important role. The model contains equations for Canadian output, prices, the stock of money (defined as M1), and interest rates.

The archetypical Canadian single-equation model of inflation would be an expectations-augmented Phillips curve of the following form:

inflation = inflation expectations + $a * f$ (output gap) + b (lagged change in the real exchange rate) + c (lagged change in indirect taxes) + d (lagged change in food prices) + e (lagged change in energy prices) + residual error.

In estimating such an equation, particular attention has been focused on the formation of inflation expectations and the measurement and relevant function of the output gap.

Until the last five years, most work at the Bank of Canada modeled inflation expectations as backward looking, with the sum of the coefficients equal to 1. But when inflation varies around a constant target, the inflation process no longer has a unit root. Then it is inappropriate to model expectations with the unit restriction on the sum of the coefficients. As one moves from one inflation regime to another, one would expect a learning process to occur, and thus the appropriate formulation for inflation expectations is quite complicated. Initial steps in modeling such a learning process (as it applies to the actual evolution of Canadian inflation) have been undertaken by Laxton, Ricketts, and Rose (1994) and Ricketts and Rose (1995) using a Markov switching process with three inflation regimes. Fillion and Léonard (1997) have used regimes similar to those captured in the Markov switching work in estimating a quarterly Phillips curve. Their model, which follows closely the archetypical model above, has inflation expectations in the current monetary regime that are close to 0.39 g(lagged inflation) + 0.61(inflation target).

Potential output and, therefore, the output gap are not easily measured. The Bank of Canada has moved from estimating potential output as a linear trend, to constructing it using a Hodrick-Prescott filter on actual output, to estimating it using a multivariate filter. The current procedure, which closely follows Butler (1996), decomposes potential output into the trend marginal product of labor, times the population, times one minus the trend unemployment rate, times the trend labor force participation rate, times the trend number of hours worked, divided by the trend of the labor share. Multivariate filters are used to estimate each trend.

The Bank of Canada has long been interested in developing structural macroeconomic models and using them for economic projections. The emphasis on structural models results from three main beliefs. The first is that economic theory and empirical work suggest the major elements in the monetary transmission mechanism. The second is that some of the major relationships in the economy are sufficiently stable that it is sensible to base an estimated or calibrated model on them. The third is that, in order to conduct policy to achieve an inflation target (or other nominal target), one must have a way of quantifying the link between current changes in interest rates and future values of the targeted variable. In September 1993 the QPM was introduced as the Bank of Canada's projection model (see Poloz, Rose, and Tetlow, 1994, and Longworth and Freedman, 1995).

It is important to note that the use of structural models for economic projections has always been supplemented by judgment, particularly in the first few quarters of the projection. Judgmental adjustments include those based on information from variables that do not enter explicitly into the structural model, such as the monetary aggregates.

Conclusion

Over the years, the management of the Bank of Canada has developed a view of how the Canadian economy works, as well as processes that help in using this view effectively in the conduct of monetary policy. Perhaps six elements are of particular importance in this regard:

- *Have a clear target.* Be explicit about the definition of the target and the target horizon.

- *Have a clear view about the monetary policy transmission mechanism.* Be explicit about the roles of real short-term interest rates, the real exchange rate, money, and credit. Be aware of the major shocks that have typically affected aggregate demand and inflation.

- *Decide which channels are the best ones to exploit in achieving the inflation target over time.* Distinguish among the aggregate demand (output gap) channel, the expectations channel, and the exchange rate pass-through channel. Do not assume much credibility to begin with.

- *Keep the forecasting models small and simple, especially at first.* Concentrate research on small to medium-size models that contain the features needed for the conduct of monetary policy. Impose theoretical restrictions when appropriate, as well as other suitable priors.

- *Actively monitor incoming data between quarterly projections.* Exploit information that is not in the quarterly model, including monetary aggregates, credit aggregates, measures of the output gap, and measures of expected inflation. Attempt to determine what the rate of underlying inflation is.

- *Use judgment to supplement the results of the models.* This is especially important in the first few quarters.

References

Armour, J., J. Atta-Mensah, W. Engert, and S. Hendry, 1996, "A Distant-Early-Warning Model of Inflation Based on M1 Disequilibria," Bank of Canada Working Paper 96–5 (Ottawa: Bank of Canada).

Black, R., T. Macklem, and D. Rose, 1998, "On Policy Rules for Price Stability," in *Price Stability, Inflation Targets, and Monetary Policy*, Proceedings of a conference held by the Bank of Canada, May 1997 (Ottawa: Bank of Canada).

Butler, L., 1996, *The Bank of Canada's New Quarterly Projection Model: Part 4CA Semi-Structural Method to Estimate Potential Output: Combining Economic Theory with a Time-Series Filter*, Bank of Canada Technical Report No. 77 (Ottawa: Bank of Canada).

Clinton, K., and D. Howard, 1994, *From Monetary Policy Instruments to Administered Interest Rates: The Transmission Mechanism in Canada*, Bank of Canada Technical Report No. 69 (Ottawa: Bank of Canada).

Clinton, K., and M. Zelmer, 1997, *Constraints on the Conduct of Canadian Monetary Policy in the 1990s: Dealing with Uncertainty in Financial Markets*, Bank of Canada Technical Report No. 80 (Ottawa: Bank of Canada).

Duguay, P., 1994, "Empirical Evidence on the Strength of the Monetary Transmission Mechanism in Canada: An Aggregate Approach," *Journal of Monetary Economics*, Vol. 33, pp. 39–61.

Fillion, J.F., and A. Léonard, 1997. "La courbe de Phillips au Canada: Un examen de quelques hypothèses." Bank of Canada Working Paper 97–3 (Ottawa: Bank of Canada).

Laflèche, T., 1996–97, "The Impact of Exchange Rate Movements on Consumer Prices," *Bank of Canada Review*, pp. 21–32.

Laxton, D., N. Ricketts, and D. Rose, 1994, "Uncertainty, Learning and Policy Credibility," in *Economic Behaviour and Policy Choice Under Price Stability*, proceedings of a conference held at the Bank of Canada, October 1993 (Ottawa: Bank of Canada).

Longworth, D., and C. Freedman, 1995, "The Role of the Staff Economic Projection in Conducting Canadian Monetary Policy," in *Targeting Inflation*, ed. by Andrew G. Haldane (London: Bank of England).

Longworth, D., and S. Poloz, 1986, *Comparison of Alternative Monetary Policy Regimes in a Small Dynamic Open-Economy Simulation Model*, Bank of Canada Technical Report No. 42 (Ottawa: Bank of Canada).

Poloz, S., D. Rose, and R. Tetlow, 1994, "The Bank of Canada's New Quarterly Projection Model (QPM): An Introduction," *Bank of Canada Review*, pp. 23–38.

Ricketts, N., and D. Rose, 1995, "Inflation, Learning and Monetary Policy Regimes in the G–7 Economies," Bank of Canada Working Paper 95–6 (Ottawa: Bank of Canada).

6 Inflation Targeting and Output Stabilization in Australia

Guy Debelle[1]

Inflation targeting has been adopted as the framework for monetary policy in a number of countries, including Australia, over the past decade. The adoption of a framework that focuses explicitly on inflation reflects the growing realization that the major contribution that monetary policy can make to economic growth and welfare in the long run is the maintenance of a low and stable inflation rate. Empirical evidence confirms the detrimental effects of higher inflation on economic growth.

However, some have criticized inflation targeting for its perceived focus on inflation as the only goal for monetary policy, to the exclusion of other goals, most notably output (see, for example, Friedman and Kuttner, 1996). Although the empirical evidence suggests the absence of a trade-off between inflation and output in the long run, there is ample evidence of a trade-off in the short run. The short-run trade-off, often represented by the short-run Phillips curve, implies a trade-off between output variability and inflation variability. Thus an exclusive focus on returning inflation to the target rate as quickly as possible may come at the expense of excessive volatility in output.

Given that the ultimate goal of policy is not inflation stabilization per se but rather welfare maximization, is inflation targeting too narrow a framework for monetary policy? Does inflation targeting pay sufficient attention to output stabilization, as, for example, a nominal income targeting framework might? This chapter considers these questions, drawing on the existing theoretical and empirical literature as well as Australia's recent experience with inflation targeting. The chapter argues that inflation targeting does take output stabiliza-

---

[1]The views expressed are those of the author and not necessarily those of the Reserve Bank of Australia.

tion into account. In general, the inflation targeting framework has sufficient flexibility to allow policymakers to make use of the short-run trade-off between output and inflation. The extent to which it does so in part reflects certain design features of the inflation targeting framework, such as targeting bands and the choice of policy horizon, that have been adopted in practice in the inflation targeting countries. Medium-term price stability can be maintained while still allowing some degree of short-run inflation variability, thus providing scope for lower output variability.

The Trade-off Between Output Variability and Inflation Variability

The role of output stabilization in inflation targeting depends crucially on the nature and length of lags in the impact of monetary policy on the economy. In many economies, changes in interest rates first affect output and then affect inflation indirectly through the effect of interest rates on the output gap. These effects take place with different lags, which in turn give rise to a trade-off between output variability and inflation variability. The interaction between output and inflation and the consequent effects on the variability of each can be illustrated by considering the impact of demand and supply shocks on the economy.[2]

First, consider a positive demand shock that increases output above its potential, leading to an increase in inflation. The policy response in this case is to increase interest rates to counteract the inflationary impulse. The extent to which interest rates are adjusted will depend on the weight that the central bank gives to output stabilization in its policy deliberations. The larger the weight given to output stability, the smaller the interest rate response. A smaller interest rate response decreases the variability in output but increases the extent to which inflation remains above the target, which implies increased variability in inflation.

The variability trade-off arises because of the differing lags between the impact of a change in interest rates on output and the impact on inflation. Absent the lag structure, output stabilization concerns would be irrelevant in the case of a demand shock: interest rates would be adjusted to close the output gap, returning output and inflation to their targets immediately. There would then be no trade-off between output variability and inflation variability.

---

[2]These issues are considered in greater detail in Svensson (1997) and Ball (1997).

In the case of a supply shock that increases inflation only, output remains at potential. Regardless of the lag structure, there is then a trade-off between output variability and inflation variability. A negative output gap is required to return inflation to its target rate. The larger the output gap generated, the quicker inflation returns to target, thereby decreasing inflation variability but at the expense of increased output variability.

Demand shocks and small supply shocks can be accommodated by appropriate design of the inflation targeting framework (as discussed below). However, large negative supply shocks that result in a large increase in the price level and the inflation rate, and possibly open up a negative output gap, create more difficulties for the policymaker. Some trade-off between inflation variability and output variability is unavoidable.

The trade-off between inflation variability and output variability can be made more stark in an open-economy context where the transmission of changes in monetary policy to inflation is particularly rapid. For example, changes in short-term interest rates may result in immediate changes in the exchange rate, which are rapidly passed through to consumer prices. In response to a deviation of inflation from target, interest rates could be adjusted by an amount large enough to engender a sufficient movement in the exchange rate to return inflation to its target rate almost immediately. Although this might be feasible, it may not be desirable, if (as is the case in many countries) the required movements in interest rates and the exchange rate are destabilizing for the real economy.

In conclusion, output stabilization clearly has a role to play in inflation targeting. The critical question is how large a role should it have. This is essentially an empirical issue.

Evidence on the Trade-off

A growing body of empirical work examines the trade-off between output variability and inflation variability.[3] For example, Stevens and Debelle (1995) estimate a simple model of the Australian economy and, by varying the weight that the central bank attaches to output stabilization, obtain the trade-off curve between output variability and inflation variability depicted in Figure 1.

As Figure 1 shows, the trade-off between inflation variability and output variability is convex. Increasing the weight that the central bank places on out-

---

[3]An early paper examining the trade-off was Taylor (1979). The volume edited by Bryant, Hooper, and Mann (1993) examines the issue extensively.

Figure 1
Inflation Variability and Output Variability

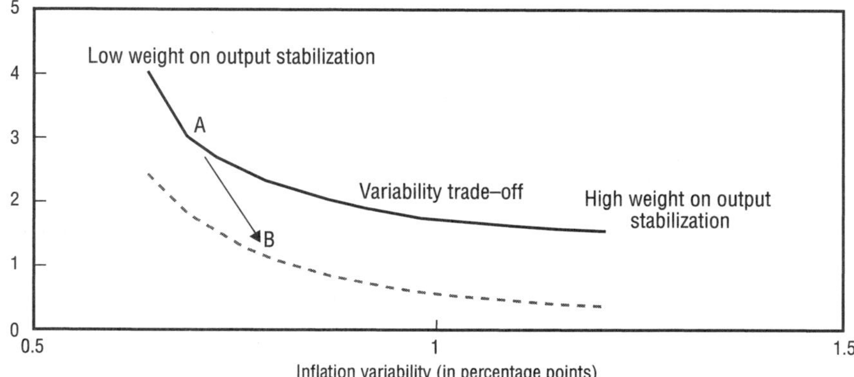

Source: Stevens and Debelle (1995).

put stabilization (moving southeast on the curve) increases the variability of inflation all along the curve while reducing the variability of output. But because the curve is convex, when a low weight is placed on output stabilization initially, small increases in that weight significantly decrease the variability of output at little cost in terms of increased variability of inflation. Also, a large range of weights on output stabilization deliver very similar outcomes for inflation variability and output variability. These are clustered around the part of the trade-off curve closest to the origin. Major differences occur only when very large weights are put on either inflation stabilization or output stabilization. These conclusions have been found for a range of countries.

In deciding on the appropriate weight to put on output stabilization, the following consideration should also be borne in mind. The initial choice on the variability frontier may influence the speed with which the central bank acquires credibility, and hence the choices available to it in the longer term (that is, the long-run position of the trade-off curve). A point such as A in Figure 1, which aims for lower inflation variability, may enable a central bank to establish its inflation-fighting credentials earlier than one that aims for lower output variability. As its credibility becomes established, the central bank might then be able to follow a more flexible approach (point B), potentially on a variability frontier closer to the origin.

The empirical literature has generally supported these theoretical conclusions: sizable gains can be achieved in terms of output stability at the cost of only a small increase in inflation variability when a more flexible approach to inflation targeting is pursued. In addition, because output is a major determinant of future inflation, placing a positive weight on output stabilization in the central bank's reaction function will always improve inflation outcomes over a reaction function that responds only to inflation. This is true regardless of whether a strict or a flexible inflation targeting regime is being pursued.

Inflation Targeting as Practiced in Australia

The formal statement of the Reserve Bank of Australia's inflation target is contained in the Statement on the Conduct of Monetary Policy,[4] signed jointly by the governor of the Reserve Bank and the treasurer of the Australian government. It defines the target as "keeping underlying inflation between 2 and 3 percent, on average, over the [business] cycle," and goes on to note that "this formulation allows for the natural short run variation in underlying inflation over the cycle while preserving a clearly identifiable benchmark performance over time."[5]

This statement highlights three aspects of an inflation targeting framework that have an impact on the degree of output stabilization: the choice of a range or a point target for inflation, the focus on the medium term, and the specification of an underlying measure of inflation. The first aspect of an inflation targeting framework that permits some degree of output stabilization is the choice between a point target and a targeting band and, if a band is chosen, its width. Specifying a target band allows for the imperfect control of monetary policy over the inflation rate. Given the long and variable lags of monetary policy, and given the impossibility of perfectly forecasting future inflation, it is not possible to restrict the variability of inflation below some minimum level. In addition to allowing for this irreducible variability in inflation, the specification of a wider band allows directly for increased scope for output stabilization.

However, the worldwide experience with inflation targeting to date suggests that inflation variability may be lower now than in the past. Thus the amount of variability in inflation that is truly irreducible may be lower than these estimates suggest, allowing the possibility that a target band could be specified

---

[4]The statement can be viewed on the Reserve Bank of Australia's World Wide Web site: www.rba.gov.au.

[5]The target has recently been changed to focus on the headline inflation rate, reflecting the recent redefinition of the consumer price index (CPI) to exclude mortgage interest charges. Nevertheless, the short-run effect on the CPI of events such as indirect tax changes are "looked through" for policy purposes.

that is both believable and attainable, without compromising the objective of output stabilization.

The choice of band width involves a trade-off between credibility and flexibility. A narrow band can be announced with hard edges that are breached occasionally, or a wide band can be specified, guaranteeing that the target will not be breached but possibly undermining the overall credibility of the framework. A narrower band (or, at the extreme, a point target) may be regarded as a stronger commitment to the inflation target.

In Australia's case, the specification of the target allows for increased flexibility. Effectively, the target specifies a "thick point" for inflation. Initially this decision was perceived as indicating weakness on the Reserve Bank's part, particularly in comparison with other inflation targeting countries. However, the experience of the past six years suggests that such concerns were misplaced.

A second aspect of the framework that can allow scope for output stabilization is the policy horizon. The longer the time frame allowed to the central bank to return inflation to the target, the greater weight it can give to output stabilization. Again, this raises the issue of the trade-off between credibility and flexibility. If the policy horizon is too long, the central bank may have trouble convincing the public that it is committed to returning inflation to its targeted rate eventually in the event of a deviation. In Australia's case, the medium-term nature of the inflation target has allowed consideration to be given to output stabilization. A notable example of this is the response of monetary policy in Australia to the Asian crisis (Stevens, 1999). The depreciation that occurred at that time was expected to lead to some increase in inflation, but not much over 3 percent. The expected decline in output growth argued against a tightening in policy. Consequently, interest rates remained unchanged until late 1998, when they were lowered by 25 basis points. The Reserve Bank's press release at the time of this easing stated that "the continuing good inflation performance, and the economy's capacity to grow without generating additional inflationary pressure, mean that it is appropriate to offer some additional support to growth through the adoption of a more accommodative monetary policy stance."

Third, the definition of the price index to be used as the target can increase the scope for output stabilization. Most inflation targeting countries focus on an underlying, or core, inflation measure as the operational target. This serves to exclude nonmonetary determinants of inflation. In New Zealand this exclusion has taken the form of prespecified "caveats," which define certain events, such as natural disasters and indirect tax changes, whose effects are excluded from the calculation of the target inflation rate.

Failure to exclude such occurrences would increase the variability of output. For example, consider an increase in indirect taxes on goods and services, which leads to an increase in their prices, raising inflation above the target range. By focusing on the underlying inflation rate, the central bank would not try to offset the first-round effect of the price rise by causing a contraction in activity. Rather, it would tolerate the increase but seek to ensure that inflation expectations do not rise as a result.

Finally, the experience of all the inflation targeting countries has demonstrated that the central bank needs to communicate clearly to the public the reasons for its policy actions. Greater public understanding about what the central bank is doing, and why, will help to increase policy credibility, particularly in the event of a deviation from the target. Increased credibility can improve the variability trade-off by ensuring that inflation expectations do not adjust rapidly to inflation shocks. The advantage of a clearly articulated inflation target is that it provides a framework within which the central bank can explain its actions.

Conclusion

Inflation targeting has sometimes been criticized for being "inflation only" targeting and ignoring output considerations. This chapter has argued that such criticism is misplaced. From a theoretical perspective, even if a strict inflation target is adopted, output considerations are still important because of the critical role that output plays in determining future inflation. The central bank will still have output in its reaction function. The argument is better framed in terms of the weight that should be placed on output stabilization in the central bank's objectives, that is, how flexible the inflation targeting regime should be.

The countries that have pursued inflation targets have adopted flexible regimes. The decision to pursue a more flexible approach reflects the shape of the inflation variability–output variability trade-off in most countries. Generally, starting from a position of strict inflation targeting, one can adopt a more flexible approach without dramatically increasing inflation variability, while simultaneously benefiting from large reductions in output variability.

The design of the inflation targeting framework also affects the degree of output stabilization that can be achieved. The use of an underlying or core measure of the inflation rate, the adoption of measures to enhance credibility (including frequent and transparent communication with the public), and the choice of policy horizon all affect the trade-off available to policymakers. Such issues, however, introduce a trade-off between flexibility and credibility. Too flexible a regime may undermine the public's confidence in the regime as a whole. Too rigid a regime may result in unnecessary output variability. However, in deciding on the appropriate degree of flexibility to adopt, consideration must be given to establishing credibility as early as possible, to allow greater flexibility in the longer run.

References

Ball, Laurence M., 1997, "Efficient Rules for Monetary Policy," NBER Working Paper No. 5952. Cambridge, Massachusetts: National Bureau of Economic Research.

Bryant, Ralph, Peter Hooper, and Catherine Mann, eds., 1993, *Evaluating Policy Regimes: New Research in Empirical Macroeconomics* (Washington: Brookings Institution).

Friedman, Benjamin M., and Kenneth N. Kuttner, 1996, "A Price Target for U.S. Monetary Policy? Lessons from the Experience with Money Growth Targets," *Brookings Papers on Economic Activity*, Vol. 1, pp. 77–146.

Stevens, Glenn, 1999, "Six Years of Inflation Targeting," *Bulletin,* Reserve Bank of Australia, May, pp. 46–61.

————, and Guy Debelle, 1995, "Monetary Policy Goals for Inflation in Australia," in *Targeting Inflation*, ed. by Andrew Haldane (London: Bank of England).

Svensson, Lars E.O., 1997, "Inflation Forecast Targeting: Implementing and Monitoring Inflation Targets," *European Economic Review*, Vol. 41, No. 6, pp. 1111–46.

Taylor, John, 1979, "Estimation and Control of a Macroeconomic Model with Rational Expectations," *Econometrica*, Vol. 47, pp. 1267–86.

7

Targeting Inflation: The United Kingdom in Retrospect

Andrew Haldane[1]

When it adopted inflation targeting in September 1992, the United Kingdom had involuntarily exited from its fixed exchange rate regime and had experienced a sharp currency depreciation as a result. The macroeconomic background was one of high and rising inflation expectations but a contracting real economy. The initial conditions for inflation targeting were not, therefore, particularly propitious.

Despite this unfavorable backdrop, the United Kingdom's experience with inflation targeting has been relatively successful so far. Retail price inflation has averaged 3 percent per year since 1993, and since 1997 it has been at or slightly above the Bank of England's target of 2.5 percent. Inflation expectations, derived from the difference in yields between nominal and inflation-indexed bonds, have been anchored at around 2.5 percent for over a year. What factors, conjunctural and institutional, have contributed to this success story?

The Impact of Devaluation

At the beginning of September 1992, inflation expectations along the entire term structure stood at around 4½ percent a year. By the end of that month, following the pound sterling's exit from the European Exchange Rate Mechanism (ERM), they had risen to 6 percent 10 years ahead, and 7 percent 20 years ahead. The loss of credibility was thus instantaneous. In the event, however, those pessimistic expectations were confounded. Although the value of sterling fell 15 percent, the pass-through of import prices at the retail level was limited. And given the weak first-round effect, there was little scope for a

---

[1]The views expressed are those of the author and not necessarily those of the Bank of England.

second-round wage-price dynamic to take hold. What accounted for the limited pass-through and the short-circuiting of the wage-price spiral? Are there lessons for other countries?

Figure 1 plots a sequence of price levels in the United Kingdom—the effective exchange rate, imported materials prices, total input prices, total output prices, and retail prices—each indexed to September 1992. These prices trace out the supply chain linkages through which one would expect a depreciation of sterling to be passed through to retail prices. Exchange rate pass-through will fail to occur, however, if the margins of the various suppliers are compressed following the devaluation. For example, a compression of foreign exporters' margins—say, because they price to market—would limit pass-through of the exchange rate change to import prices. A compression of domestic wholesalers' margins would limit pass-through from domestic input

Figure 1

United Kingdom: Exchange Rates and Selected Price Indices Following Exit from the ERM

(index, Aug 1992 = 100)

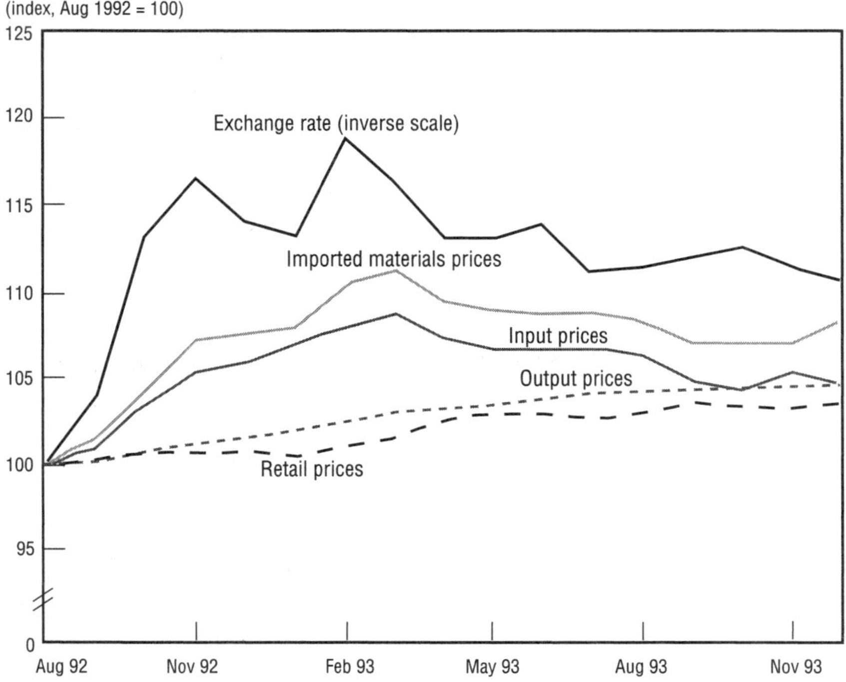

Source: Bank of England data.

prices to output prices. Finally, a compression of retailers' margins would limit pass-through between output prices and retail prices.

Events immediately following sterling's exit from the ERM suggest some compression in all of these margins. An endogenous supply-side response limited first-round pass-through. This appears to have resulted from the depressed state of domestic demand in the United Kingdom at the time, which left suppliers unable to raise prices for fear of further depressing demand and losing market share. This pattern of limited pass-through was repeated in many other countries in the 1990s that experienced sharp depreciations, such as Australia, Finland, and Sweden.

The Institutional Framework and the Inflation Target

The institutional framework for inflation targeting in the United Kingdom has evolved during the period the regime has been in place but is now set out explicitly in the Bank of England Act of 1998. This legislation gives the Bank of England instrument independence, to be exercised by a nine-person Monetary Policy Committee (MPC). The inflation target itself is set by the government; thus the MPC is goal-dependent. The MPC meets monthly to decide interest rates. The minutes of its deliberations are published, together with the votes of individual members, with a two-week lag. Several other vehicles ensure the accountability and transparency of the MPC's decisions. These include the publication of a quarterly *Inflation Report*, summarizing the Bank of England's inflation assessment; a mandatory open letter to the Chancellor of the Exchequer in the event inflation breaches the target by more than 1 percentage point in either direction; and appearances by members of the MPC before parliamentary committees.

The move to instrument independence, first announced in May 1997, prompted an immediate fall of 50 basis points (half a percentage point) along the entire term structure of U.K. inflation expectations. The published minutes, the *Inflation Report,* and the parliamentary committee appearances expose the MPC's analysis to a powerful external discipline. Besides meeting a democratic demand for accountability, these measures have increased internal incentives within the Bank of England to maintain and improve the quality of its analysis.

The effects of greater transparency in monetary policy are already evident in the yield curve. Transparency has increased the predictability of the short end of the yield curve, in particular, at the time of monetary policy changes. For example, during the period when sterling operated within the ERM, the average "surprise" in three-month interest rates following a 1-percentage-point rise in official rates was around 50 basis points. Over the period of inflation targeting, the average surprise has fallen to around 12 basis points. And interestingly, since May 1997, when the MPC was formed, the average surprise has been lower still, at 10 basis points. This suggests that the move to inflation targeting has been associated with a significant damping in yield curve uncertainty. It also suggests that, contrary to the predictions of some outside commentators, a committee-based approach to policy setting, with individual votes expressed and published, has not reduced the predictability of monetary policy actions in the United Kingdom.

The centerpiece of the United Kingdom's monetary framework is a point target for annual inflation of 2.5 percent. The choice of this figure is dictated by several factors, including the well-known measurement biases in price indices and the recognition that some of the costs of inflation—such as those associated with imperfect indexation of the tax system—may be nontrivial even at low inflation rates. Importantly, however, an inflation rate of 2–3 percent also seems fairly well aligned with the inflation preferences of the U.K. general public. Public acceptability is an important factor in ensuring the ongoing legitimacy of any country's monetary framework, especially in its early stages.

The choice of an inflation point target rather than a range serves several purposes. Most important, it removes any ambiguity about what monetary policy should be set relative to, and hence it anchors inflation expectations. For example, between 1992 and 1995 the United Kingdom operated with an inflation target range of 1–4 percent rather than a point target. A "range bias" appeared to exist throughout this period, with inflation expectations implied from the yield curve fixed at around the top of the range. The inflation target appears to have been seen as a "range of indifference" for policymakers over this period. Since 1995 and the move to a point inflation target, inflation expectations have fallen steadily, as range bias has been ironed out.

A further benefit of a point inflation target is that it makes transparent the symmetry of monetary policy actions. An inflation targeting framework is as much a safeguard against deflation as against inflation. Symmetry is a desirable characteristic of any steady-state inflation target. It is not generally desirable, however, for monetary policy to behave in this symmetric fashion during the transition to low inflation. Along the disinflationary path, an asymmetric, or "opportunistic," approach to monetary policy is often more appropriate.

What this means in practice is that adverse inflation outcomes are still vigorously offset through monetary policy, but favorable inflation shocks are instead accommodated. The reason for this asymmetry in response is that reflating the economy following a favorable inflation shock would mean inflicting a further disinflation on the economy at some later stage. Rather than do this, it may be better to pocket the lucky inflation shock—to seize the opportunity—and accept temporary overachievement of the inflation target. Many countries in recent years, including Israel most recently, have found themselves needing to behave in this asymmetric fashion.

Inflation Forecast Targeting

At root, the monetary policy rule under inflation targeting can be simplified to:

$$E_t \, \pi_{t+j} \mid i_t = \pi^*,$$

where $E_t \, \pi_{t+j}$ is the expectation, based on information available at time t, of the inflation rate j periods ahead, conditioned on some path for the nominal interest rate $(. \mid i_t)$, and π^* is the inflation target. So under inflation targeting, monetary policy aims to align the forecast of inflation j periods ahead with the inflation target. In effect, it practices inflation forecast targeting.

Inflation forecast targeting clearly raises some technical questions. For example, how does monetary policy deal with forecast uncertainties? What is the appropriate targeting horizon (that is, what value for j)? And how does one accommodate output smoothing? Inflation forecast uncertainties are significant even among the established inflation targets. There are two aspects to dealing with these inflation uncertainties, one ex ante, the other ex post.

The Bank of England makes clear the extent of ex ante inflation forecast uncertainties by constructing a probability density function, or fan chart, for inflation forecast outcomes up to two years ahead. This is published in the quarterly *Inflation Report*. (A fan chart for forecast output growth is published as well.) The published distribution illustrates the MPC's views of both the variance of likely inflation outcomes and any potential skews or asymmetric risks to inflation. The distribution quantifies these uncertainties and skews; it deemphasizes point inflation forecasts, since these are almost certain to be incorrect ex post; and it thereby allows explicitly probabilistic statements to be made about monetary policy. For example, it allows (conditioned on the assumption of unchanged nominal interest rates) statements such as "there is an x percent probability of inflation lying between y percent and z percent two years ahead." This probabilistic approach may be particularly useful at times of significant inflation uncertainty, or when the balance of inflation risks is highly asymmetric.

There is also, however, an ex post dimension—that is, an accountability rather than a transparency dimension—to dealing with inflation uncertainties. Shocks are certain to push inflation away from the target, even if only temporarily. An independent central bank (the agent) needs to be able to explain those deviations to the government and the public (the principal). The United

Kingdom operates an open letter system to meet this demand for accountability. If inflation deviates from the target by 1 percentage point or more in either direction, the MPC writes a published letter to the chancellor explaining why the deviation has occurred and describing what the MPC intends to do to offset it and over what time horizon. However, the choice of an appropriate time horizon for inflation targeting also raises a number of technical questions.

Fundamentally, the optimal forecast horizon under inflation targeting depends on two factors: the length of monetary transmission lags (a "technology" constraint), and policymakers' output and inflation preferences (a "taste" constraint). Taking lags first, simulations in the United Kingdom suggest that monetary policy has its maximum marginal effect on output after around one year, and on inflation after around two years. This stylized fact helps justify the Bank of England's choice of a forecast horizon of around two years.

On the issue of output and inflation preferences, longer forecast horizons allow a more graduated monetary policy response following inflation shocks, and hence allow greater output smoothing. Using policy simulations, it is possible to trace out a trade-off between inflation variability and output variability, defined in terms of different inflation forecast horizons. Shorter horizons push one toward the end of the trade-off where inflation variability is low and output variability high. The optimal point on the trade-off, based on a calibration for the United Kingdom, suggests a forecast horizon of around 18 months to two years.

Dealing with the Exchange Rate

A key issue for inflation targeting countries, as small, open economies, is how monetary policy should respond to movements in the exchange rate. This becomes a particularly thorny issue following a sharp exchange rate depreciation, like that the United Kingdom faced in September 1992.

The Bank of England's approach to dealing with the exchange rate problem has been to try to identify the underlying source of the exchange rate shock. For example, is the shock real or monetary in nature? Is it domestic or foreign in origin? Is it temporary or permanent? Without answers to these questions, it becomes very difficult to determine the effects of a given exchange rate movement on monetary conditions. For example, a real exchange rate shock would have very different implications for output than a monetary shock, and likewise if a shock were believed to be temporary rather than permanent.

But how are these different shocks teased apart? The Bank of England has developed a number of ways of decomposing exchange rate changes. One is to extract the proportion of a given exchange rate change that can be accounted

Figure 2
United Kingdom: Impact of Monetary Shocks on the Exchange Rate in Two Episodes

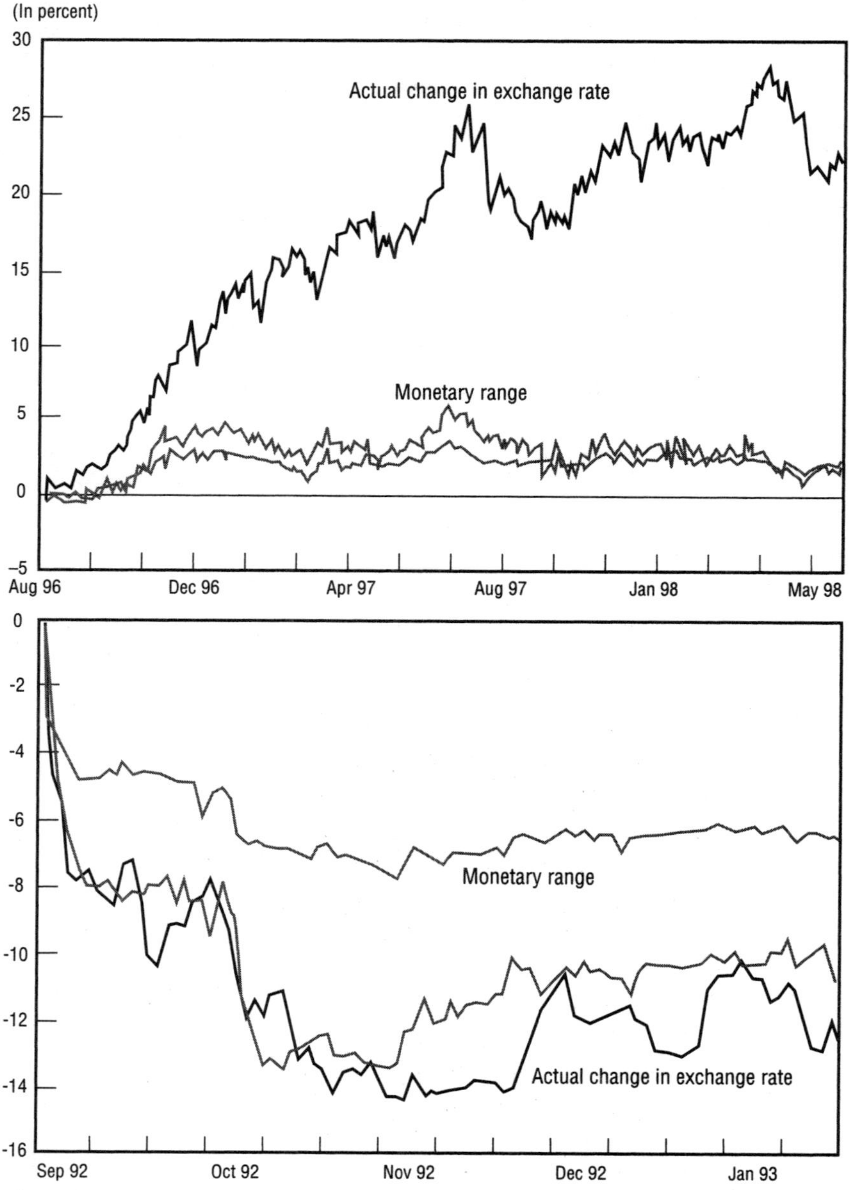

Source: Bank of England data.

for by relative yield curve movements—that is, monetary shocks—on the assumption that uncovered interest parity holds. Figure 2 offers two examples of such a decomposition: first, following sterling's appreciation between 1996 and 1998; and second, following sterling's depreciation after exiting the ERM in 1992. In the first case, monetary "news"—the rise in the U.K. yield curve relative to that overseas—can account for perhaps only around 3 percentage points of the more than 20 percent appreciation. In the second case, however, the relative easing of U.K. monetary policy following exit from the ERM plausibly accounted for most, if not all, of sterling's subsequent depreciation.

A second type of decomposition can be used to derive a measure of the foreign exchange risk premium, for example, by using survey-based measures of exchange rate expectations. Plotting the risk premium in the United Kingdom against that in the euro area over recent years shows an interesting pattern. The risk premium on sterling assets became strongly negative in the immediate runup to European monetary union, perhaps reflecting uncertainties about that process. This fall in the sterling risk premium plausibly accounted for some of the appreciation of sterling against the European currencies during this period. Subsequently, as euro-related uncertainties resolved themselves from the middle of 1998 onward, the sterling risk premium rose, and (until recently anyway) sterling fell back with it.

Risk premium effects are, by their nature, likely to be relatively shorter lived than other types of nonmonetary exchange rate disturbance. Knowing that an exchange rate movement is related to the risk premium is therefore important when gauging the durability of its effect on monetary conditions. Such analysis may therefore be a useful part of the toolkit when interpreting exchange rate movements.

8 Monetary Policy and Inflation Targeting in Chile

Felipe Morandé and Klaus Schmidt-Hebbel[1]

Inflation targeting is the new kid on the block of monetary regimes.[2] Since the early 1990s, seven industrial countries and a few emerging economies, Chile among them, have adopted inflation targeting as the cornerstone of their monetary policy. This chapter reviews the conduct of monetary policy in Chile and the role of inflation targeting in the country's gradual convergence toward price stability.[3]

The Conduct of Monetary Policy in Chile

Chile's monetary policy is anchored to an annual inflation target.[4] As part of its monetary programming, the Central Bank of Chile projects and monitors the main monetary aggregates. However, the fact that the central bank develops internal projections of monetary aggregates does not imply that these are used as intermediate targets. The same is true for the exchange rate. Although the central bank monitors exchange rate trends, the exchange rate is not an intermediate target for the conduct of monetary policy. Indeed, market forces have determined the exchange rate since September 1999, when the central bank adopted a floating exchange rate regime.

---

[1]Excellent assistance provided by Matías Tapia is gratefully acknowledged. The views expressed are those of the authors and do not necessarily represent those of the Central Bank of Chile.

[2]Among recent work on inflation targeting, its rationale, and international experience see Masson, Savastano, and Sharma (1997), Debelle and others (1998), and Bernanke and others (1999).

[3]A longer paper, related to this one, compares Chile's inflation targeting framework with those applied in other industrial and emerging economies (Landerretche, Morandé, and Schmidt-Hebbel, 2000).

[4]Detailed reviews of monetary policy and the costs of inflation in the Chilean context can be found in Massad (1998) and Marshall (1999).

Since the mid-1980s, the main operational objective of monetary policy is a real interest rate. The widespread use of explicit real interest rates in financial markets has been a market response to historically high inflation and reflects the extent of indexation in the Chilean economy. From 1985 through 1995, the rate set by monetary policy was the real rate on indexed central bank paper of 90 days maturity. The real rate is applied to the principal, which is adjusted on a daily basis by a unit of account that is indexed daily to the consumer price index with an average lag of 20 days. Since May 1995 the policy rate is the real daily rate paid on interbank loans (the real overnight interbank rate).

The Central Bank of Chile announces its policy rate publicly. Through the conduct of open market operations, the central bank guides the interbank rate toward the policy objective. Since May 1995—except for four months in 1998—the difference between the policy rate and the actual interbank rate has been only 5 basis points. Open market operations are performed by issuing central bank paper and by conducting repos (repurchase agreements) and reverse repos. A program of monthly issues of central bank paper is announced in advance, providing markets with information about the overall stance of monetary policy that is consistent with the real interest rate. Complementary repo and reverse repo operations are conducted during the month in order to satisfy the demand for liquidity at the policy rate of interest.

The central bank provides two standard facilities to financial institutions to use at their discretion: the line of liquidity credit and the liquidity deposit window. The line of liquidity credit provides central bank credit to individual institutions (subject to quantitative ceilings) at marginal interest rates that rise with the amount of the required credit to three different levels. The liquidity deposit window is an open window where financial institutions can deposit their excess liquidity at a floor interest rate. Figure 1 depicts the evolution of market interest rates (the overnight interbank rate) and policy interest rates in Chile since 1997.

From 1984 through September 1999, Chile's exchange rate policy was based on a crawling exchange rate band. The objective of the band was to provide markets with guidance about the desirable trend of the real exchange rate and reduce excessive exchange rate volatility. However, after the inception of the band, many of its features—including its central parity, its width, the rate of crawl, the reference currency basket, and the degree of symmetry—were altered in response to changing policy objectives and market conditions. In addition, intramarginal exchange interventions were frequent and at times intense.

When the exchange rate band was suspended in September 1999, the market exchange rate was close to the center of the band. This demonstrates that the adoption of a flexible exchange rate system at that time was not the result of mar-

Figure 1

Chile: Interest Rates Set by Monetary Policy and Overnight Interbank Rates

(In percent per year)

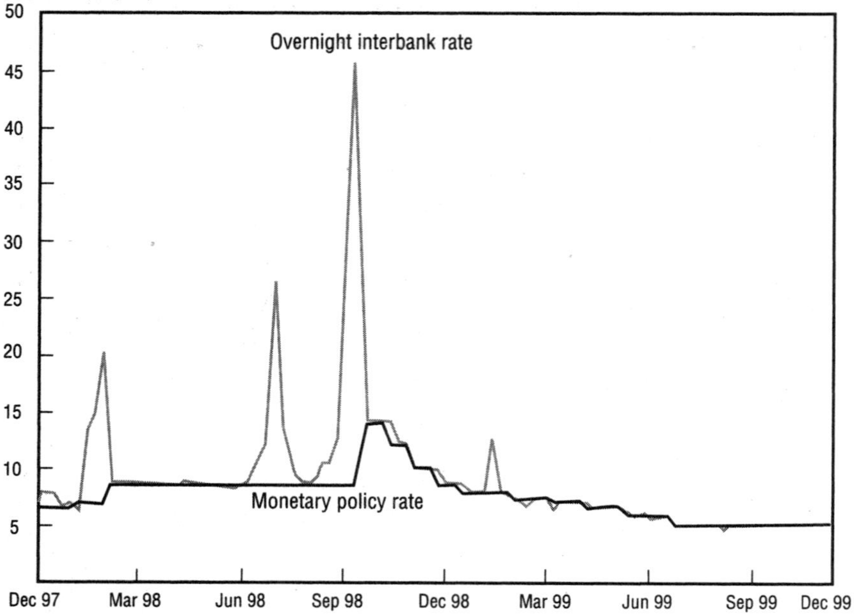

Source: Central Bank of Chile data.

ket pressures. In fact, the floating system was adopted both to allow market forces to determine the exchange rate and to strengthen the inflation targeting regime. Figure 2 depicts trends in the exchange rate band and the market exchange rate.

How does the Central Bank of Chile determine monetary policy? The main focus of the central bank's implicit monetary policy rule is on the gap between actual core inflation and the inflation target over the relevant 24-month policy horizon. In addition, a number of key variables are closely watched and projected; foremost among these is the gap between actual and potential output, which reflects current and projected future business cycle conditions. Other monitored variables that are crucial for monetary transmission and inflation in Chile include the aggregate spending-income gap (or the current account deficit), output growth, the unemployment rate, monetary growth, wage growth, the exchange rate, the fiscal policy stance, and the term structure of market interest rates.

As in other open economies, the main channels of transmission of a change in the policy rate include market interest rates and their term structure, mon-

Figure 2
Chile: Real Exchange Rate Band and Market Real Exchange Rates

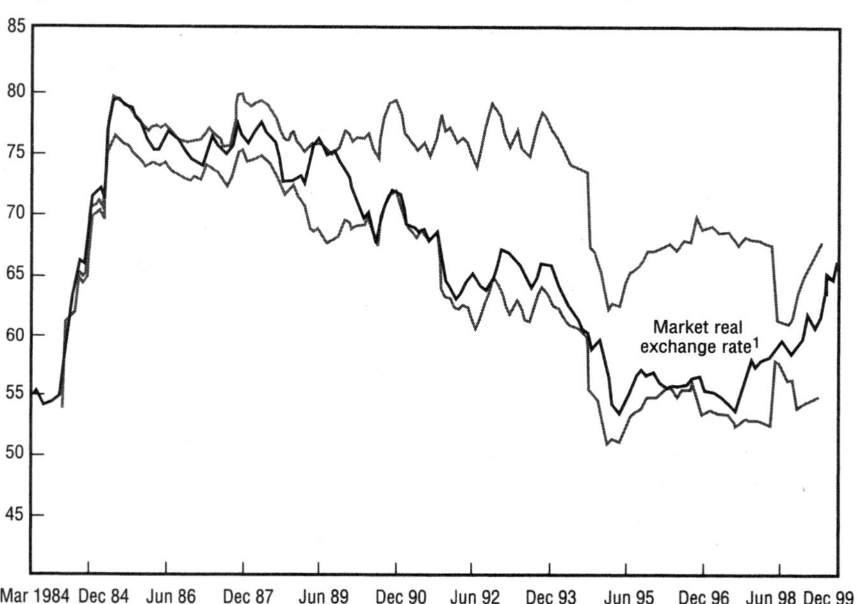

Source: Central Bank of Chile data.
Note: Lighter tracings indicate the real exchange rate band. The central parity is defined as the nominal central
parity, established by the central bank, multiplied by the ratio of the U.S. CPI to the Chilean CPI.
¹Nominal market exchange rate in pesos per dollar divided by the Chilean CPI and multiplied by the U.S. CPI
(both CPIs indexed to 1980=100).

etary and credit aggregates, and the exchange rate (Figure 3). These variables
act upon (and are affected by) macroeconomic aggregates and the prices of
goods, labor, and assets. Indexation is a structural feature of the Chilean economy that raises price inertia and slows relative price adjustment, contributing
to a faster transmission of exchange rate and wage shocks to aggregate inflation. Information about the gap between actual core inflation and the inflation
target, as well as from other macroeconomic and financial variables, feeds back
to contribute to a possible revision of the stance of monetary policy.

Inflation Targeting in Chile

Upon being granted its independence in 1990, the central bank had to face a
significant rise in inflation caused by expansionary policies in 1989 and the oil
price shock associated with the Persian Gulf war. In this context the central
bank simultaneously tightened monetary policy and decided to adopt an annual inflation target as its nominal anchor.

Figure 3
Chile: Channels of Monetary Transmission

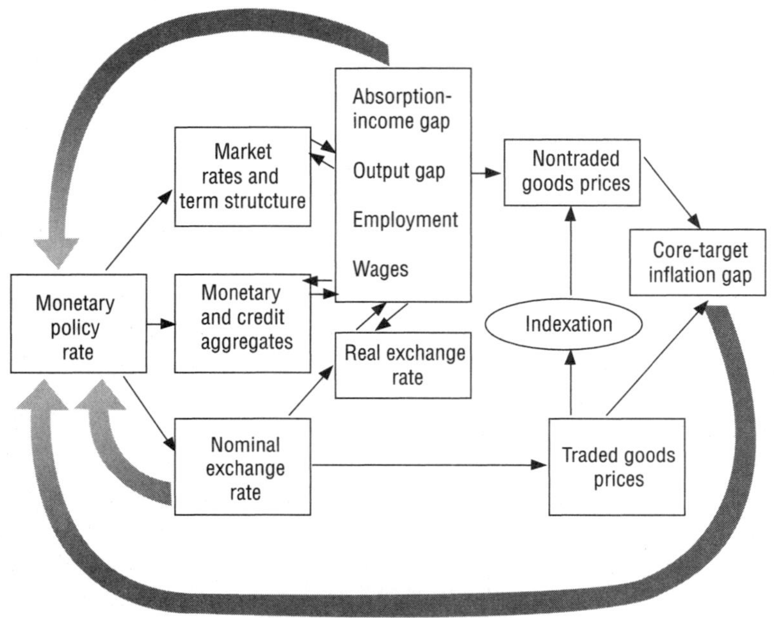

Chile's recent inflation history records two major stabilization programs, in 1959–62 and in 1979–82. Both were based on a nominal exchange rate anchor as the main instrument for stabilization, and both failed miserably. Using the exchange rate anchor for a third time to reduce inflation in Chile would have made it very difficult for the newly independent central bank to establish its credibility. On the other hand, the use of monetary aggregates as an intermediate target would also have been difficult in a country with developing financial markets and volatile money demand. The remaining choice for the nominal anchor was the inflation target. An additional explanation of Chile's early adoption of an inflation target was the notion that providing the public with an explicit inflation objective—and committing to its attainment by adopting a supportive monetary policy—would reduce the role of indexation mechanisms, hence lowering the cost of stabilization.

The first inflation target was announced in September 1990 for the 12 months of 1991. Since that first announcement, the inflation target has been generally attained with great precision. Figure 4 depicts the convergence of targeted and actual inflation from high initial levels (actual inflation was 27.3

Figure 4
Chile: Inflation Target and Actual Inflation

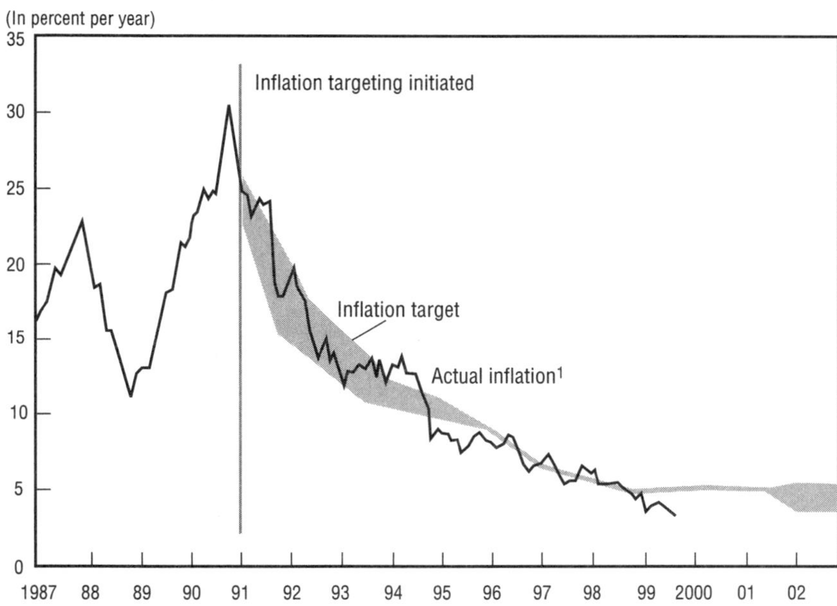

Source: Central Bank of Chile data.
[1] As measured by the consumer price index.

percent in 1990) to values consistent with low and stationary inflation (actual inflation was 2.3 percent in 1999). In September 1999 the central bank announced a point target of 3.5 percent for 2000 and a stationary target range of 2–4 percent for the indefinite future, starting in 2001.

A key feature of Chile's inflation target–based stabilization in the 1990s is its gradualness, which has contributed to reducing inflation without incurring substantial output costs. During most of the 1990s—with the exception of the 1999 recession in the aftermath of the Asian and Russian crises—Chile has grown at high rates under conditions of full employment. Real GDP growth is projected to bounce back to 5.5–6 percent in 2000.

Policy Effectiveness under Inflation Targeting

The downward path of the inflation target and the inflation rate in Chile is not definite proof that target-based monetary policy has been more effective than an alternative monetary framework would have been. For example, one might argue that, rather than acting as a credibility-enhancing commitment device, the inflation target has simply been an information-improving official inflation forecast with an excellent track record.

One way to assess the effectiveness of policy under inflation targeting is to compare inflation forecasts made prior to the announcement of the central bank's annual inflation target with that target and with actual inflation. We obtain the benchmark inflation forecasts as the out-of-sample inflation prediction based on an unrestricted vector autoregressive (VAR) model.[5] It is important to note that the model is estimated for each policy announcement using the information available through the preceding month. The forecast is simulated dynamically 16 periods ahead for each inflation target announcement.

We present the results for two VAR-based forecasts. Both VAR models include six endogenous variables (interest rates, wages, GDP, the consumer price index, the money supply, and the nominal exchange rate) and two exogenous variables (the terms of trade and the U.S. consumer price index). The models differ in that one includes a time trend (as an exogenous variable) whereas the other does not.

The results are presented in Figures 5 (with the time trend variable) and 6 (without the time trend variable). The shaded bar depicts the inflation target range or target point announced after the last period on which the out-of-sample inflation forecast (the gray line) is based. The black line depicts actual inflation.

The first and expected result is that the forecasts based on the VAR that includes a time trend are much closer to actual inflation than those based on the VAR without the time trend. This reflects the negative trend in annual inflation observed during the 1990s.

The second and main result is that forecast inflation is typically higher than either targeted or actual inflation. This suggests that the systematic attainment of declining annual inflation targets contributed to a correction of inflation expectations and forecasts. In the absence of credible September announcements of future lower inflation targets, the best (model-based) forecast of future inflation reflects a mean reversion to higher (historical) rates of inflation in the future. The results suggest that the September target announcements helped in correcting inflation forecasts downward.

The results are less clear-cut in Figure 5, where the inflation forecasts are based on the VAR model that includes a time trend. This trend is likely to

---

[5]A more extensive treatment of this exercise can be found in Landerretche, Morandé, and Schmidt-Hebbel (2000).

Figure 5

Chile: Actual Inflation and Forecasts of the VAR Model, with NER, with Trend

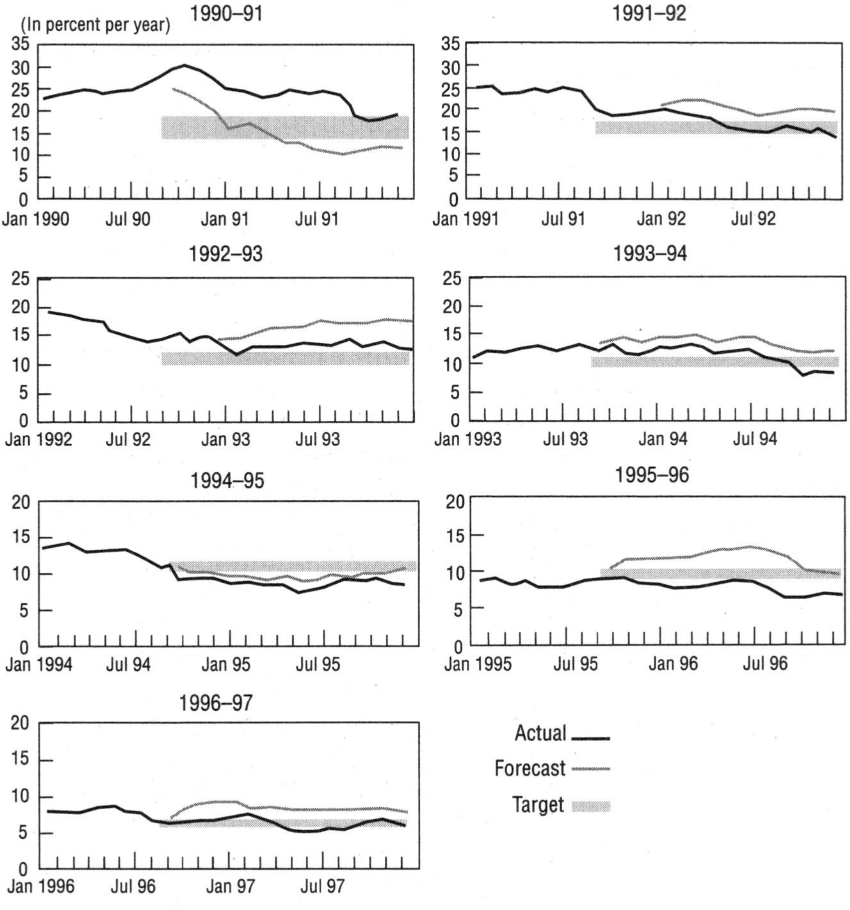

Source: Authors' calculations and Central Bank of Chile data.

proxy for the markets' expectations of a declining inflation trend, which is itself a function of the credible attainment of a declining inflation path by the central bank. In contrast, the results are very strong in Figure 6, where the forecasts are based on the VAR model that excludes the time trend. Here, in six out of seven cases, the out-of-sample forecasts show increasing divergence of inflation forecasts from both actual and target inflation rates over time. This suggests that inflation targeting has allowed a break with in-

Figure 6

Chile: Actual Inflation and Forecasts of the VAR Model, with NER, without Trend

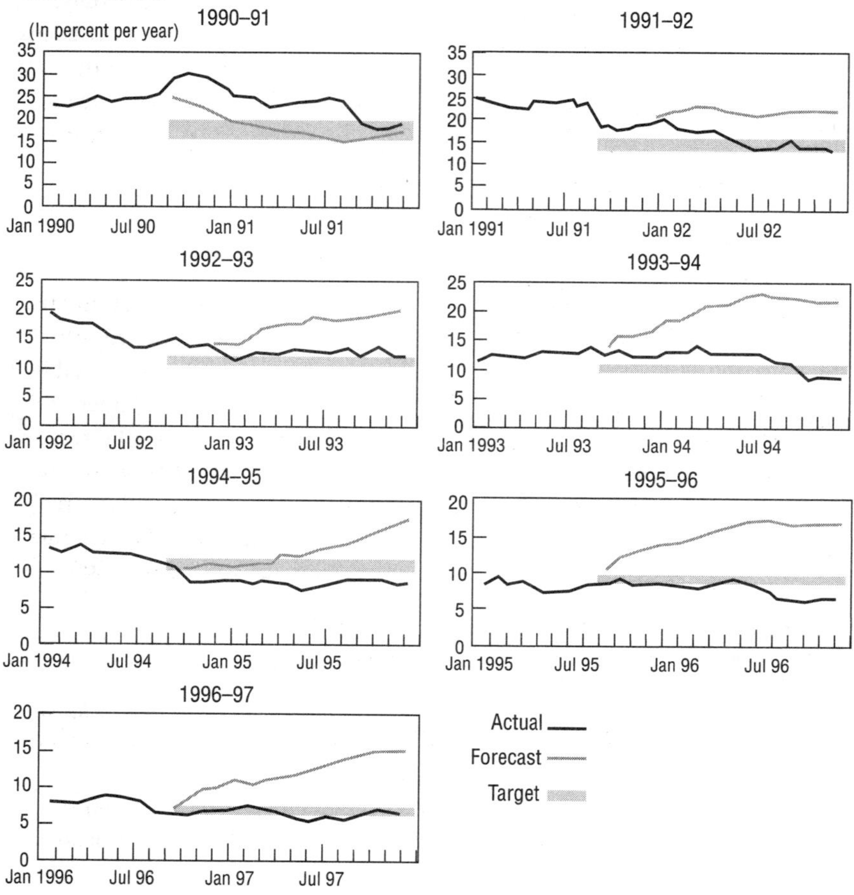

Source: Authors' calculations and Central Bank of Chile data.

flation history, leading to a gradual downward correction of actual and expected inflation.

We conclude that, for most specifications and sample periods, the inflation target was below the forecast, and actual inflation was closer to the target than to the forecast. Although these results do not provide conclusive evidence, they suggest that inflation targeting played a prominent role in reducing inflation. Indeed, a major transmission mechanism of Chile's monetary framework based on inflation targeting may be the credible announcement of the target. The use of a preannounced inflation objective by a central bank strongly committed to its achievement may have overcome the strong mean-reverting effects of inflation inertia in a country like Chile, where indexation had been widespread. The results reported here provide suggestive evidence that the inflation target has served two purposes: as a credibility-enhancing device for the conduct of monetary policy, and as an effective means of year-to-year communication of information from the central bank to the markets.

Conclusion

Chile's adoption in 1990 of a monetary policy regime based on inflation targeting has contributed to policy credibility and has supported the country's gradual convergence toward price stability. The empirical evidence reported in this chapter suggests that announcement of an explicit inflation target and adoption of a supportive monetary policy that lent credibility to the target were instrumental in breaking inflation expectations and attaining convergence toward low, stationary inflation. The monetary framework and its credibility were further strengthened by the adoption of a floating exchange rate regime in late 1999 and publication of an inflation report since May 2000.

References

Bernanke, Ben, Thomas Laubach, Frederic Mishkin, and Adam Posen, 1999, *Inflation Targeting: Lessons from the International Experience* (Princeton, New Jersey: Princeton University Press).

Debelle, Guy, Paul Masson, Miguel A. Savastano, and Sunil Sharma, 1998, "Inflation Targeting as a Framework for Monetary Policy," *Economic Issues*, International Monetary Fund (September).

Landerretche, Oscar, Felipe Morandé, and Klaus Schmidt-Hebbel, 2000, "Inflation Targets and Stabilization in Chile," in *Monetary Policy Frameworks in a Global Context*, ed. by L. Mahadeva and G. Sterne (London: Routledge).

Marshall, J., 1999, "La Política Monetaria y la Distribución del Ingreso," *Revista de Economía Chilena*, Central Bank of Chile, Vol. 2, No. 1, pp. 5–22.

Massad, C., 1998, "La Política Monetaria en Chile," *Revista de Economía Chilena*, Central Bank of Chile, Vol. 1, No. 1, pp. 7–27.

Masson, Paul, Miguel A. Savastano, and Sunil Sharma, 1997, "The Scope for Inflation Targeting in Developing Countries," *IMF Working Paper* WP/97/130, October (Washington: International Monetary Fund).

9 Inflation Targeting Under a Crawling Band Exchange Rate Regime: Lessons from Israel

Leonardo Leiderman and Gil Bufman[1]

Consider a small, open economy that, after a long period of chronically high inflation, substantial fiscal and current account deficits, and a marked accumulation of domestic and foreign debt, implements a comprehensive, exchange rate–based stabilization program. The program results in a sharp reduction in the rate of inflation to about 15–20 percent per year. Although this reduction in inflation is considered a major achievement, it is accompanied by a real appreciation of the currency and weakened export competitiveness two to three years after the stabilization, and this trend cannot be sustained over time. Given this situation, and given the increasing need to allow for some reaction of the nominal exchange rate to capital inflows and outflows, sooner or later policymakers in this hypothetical economy are likely to consider introducing some degree of exchange rate flexibility. The question is how to do so while avoiding the possible inflationary consequences of a nominal depreciation and creating the conditions for a further reduction in inflation toward world levels.

Faced with just such a policy dilemma, several countries have devised exit strategies from the regimes they adopted during the first phase of stabilization and have sought greater exchange rate flexibility in at least one of two forms: crawling exchange rate bands or explicit inflation targets. In those countries that have adopted them, crawling bands are seen as a regime that partly maintains an anchoring role for the nominal exchange rate, yet at the same time provides flexibility to deal with short-term shocks and with the marked volatility of international capital flows. Inflation targets, if credible, are seen as

---

[1]Parts of this chapter draw on the authors' previous joint work as cited in the references. The authors thank Rafi Lipa for research assistance. The views expressed in the paper are the sole responsibility of the authors.

a transparent mechanism through which the authorities can make commitments and discipline their monetary policy without necessarily incurring the macroeconomic costs of a currency peg. In some countries, such as Chile, Colombia, Israel, and Poland, the two anchors coexist.

The disinflation experience in recent years of various countries with the characteristics just described provides a rich and useful foundation for analysis of monetary policy strategies for disinflation. A leading example is Israel, where monetary policy has been based on both a crawling exchange rate band and inflation targets since 1992. Although the years from the 1985 stabilization program to 1991 were characterized by a rate of inflation averaging about 18 percent per year, in the next phase, from 1992 to 1996, annual inflation was reduced to about 10 percent on average (Figure 1). More recently there was a sharp reduction in the rate of inflation, to 7 percent in 1997, and year-over-year inflation to September 1998 was only 4.7 percent. This decline was interrupted temporarily by exchange rate–induced pressures due to the volatility in world financial markets during September–November 1998, which gave rise to a sharp depreciation of the shekel and a rise in measured inflation. However, because of tighter monetary policy and the impact of other factors, a marked drop in the rate of inflation followed, and in fact the price level fell during the first quarter of 1999. At the time of this writing (May 1999), most forecasts

Figure 1
Israel: Inflation Targets, Actual Inflation, and Market Expectations

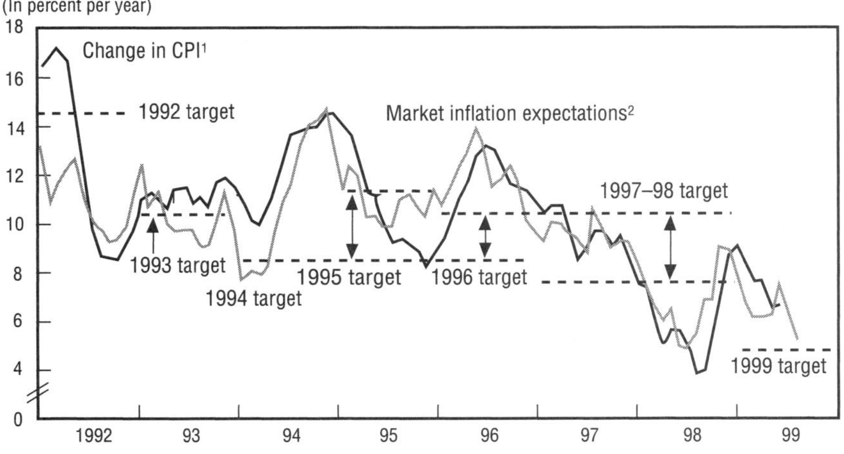

Source: Bank of Israel.
[1] Year over year.
[2] Expectation of the rate of inflation 12 months ahead.

pointed to an inflation rate below the official target of 4 percent in 1999, but to a slightly higher rate in the 12 months ahead.

This chapter documents and analyzes Israel's experience with monetary policy and disinflation, with particular emphasis on the coexistence of two nominal anchors—an exchange rate band and an inflation target—in circumstances where the fiscal policy stance is not compatible with the latter. Despite some difficulties, inflation targeting has played a very useful and important role in Israel's disinflation and has become the main anchor of nominal policies.

Israel's Experience with Inflation Targeting

Monetary policy in Israel has gone through major changes in recent years. It was highly accommodative in the late 1970s and early 1980s, supporting the escalation of inflation to triple digits. The first phase in the aftermath of the remarkable stabilization program of June 1985 featured a policy oriented toward sustaining a fixed but adjustable nominal exchange rate, which was considered a key nominal anchor in the disinflation effort. Throughout this first phase, from 1986 to 1991, inflation stayed in the range of 16–20 percent as a yearly average. The second phase, from 1992 to 1996, was characterized by the modification of the exchange rate regime to one based on a crawling exchange rate band and by the adoption of an explicit inflation target. The crawling band stipulates a rate of crawl of the central parity that is approximately equal to the difference between the inflation target and a forecast of world inflation. Currently the government announces the inflation target for a given year, after consultation with the central bank, in the second half of the preceding year, in the context of the next year's budget decisions. In this second phase the average rate of inflation was reduced to about 10 percent per year.[2]

Although it is still too early to reach a definitive conclusion, recent developments suggest that a third phase in the disinflation process began in 1997, characterized by single-digit and declining rates of inflation. As already noted, inflation was 7 percent in 1997 and 4.7 percent year-over-year to September 1998. Following a temporary acceleration of inflation from September to November 1998—mainly due to the impact of world financial developments on Israel's exchange rate and prices—inflation continued to fall. In fact, the consumer price index fell during the first quarter of 1999, quite a rare event in Is-

---

[2]For description and analysis of monetary and exchange rate policies in Israel in recent years, see Bruno (1993), Leiderman (1993), Helpman, Leiderman, and Bufman (1994), Bufman, Leiderman, and Sokoler (1995), Leiderman and Bufman (1996), and Sokoler (1997). On inflation targets, see Leiderman and Svensson (1995).

rael's inflation history, and most current forecasts point to an inflation rate for 1999 that is below the official target of 4 percent.

Although a nominal exchange rate commitment such as a crawling exchange rate band can be effective in achieving disinflation, it may give rise to certain well-known difficulties. First, any such commitment is fragile and vulnerable in a world of substantial capital mobility, where cross-border capital flows can be subject to sharp reversals. Second, a preset range for the trajectory of the nominal exchange rate can slow the process of real exchange rate adjustment to real and financial shocks. Third, the existence of a relatively narrow range for exchange rate fluctuations may lead to a distortion, in that the public might come to perceive exchange rate risk as substantially less than it is in reality. This distortion may induce large capital inflows when there is a sizable gap between domestic and foreign interest rates. Developments in Mexico and several East Asian countries before their crises in the 1990s are evidence that this can happen. Last, nominal exchange rate targeting may conflict with other objectives of macroeconomic policy, including monetary policy, such as the inflation target. In particular, it may well be that the level of the interest rate required to achieve the inflation target differs sharply from the level appropriate for sustaining the currency band. In part because of these difficulties, the policy regime in Israel has gradually shifted over the years toward increased flexibility of the nominal exchange rate (as shown by the widening of the band in Figure 2), coupled with increased emphasis on inflation targeting.

Figure 1 demonstrated the severe challenges to official inflation targets throughout the 1990s.[3] Although there are no explicit multiyear inflation targets in Israel, when the annual targets were set for both 1997 and 1998 (at 7–10 percent), the government added the objective of having an inflation target for the year 2001 similar to that common in the countries of the Organisation for Economic Co-operation and Development. It also set the objective of continuing the gradual reduction in inflation, to achieve price stability like that in these industrial countries over time. A measure of market expectations of inflation is derived from the yields on inflation-indexed and nonindexed bonds traded in the local capital market. It can be seen that there have been several periods in which inflation deviated from the target. Measured in December (year-over-year), as specified by the target, the largest such deviation occurred in 1994, when annual inflation reached 14.5 percent, compared with a target of 8 percent. However, in 1995 and 1997 the targets were achieved, and any de-

---

[3]For more detailed discussion of these and related developments, see recent issues of the Bank of Israel's *Annual Report.*

Figure 2
Israel: Exchange Rate of the Shekel and Its Target Range

(In shekels per currency basket unit)

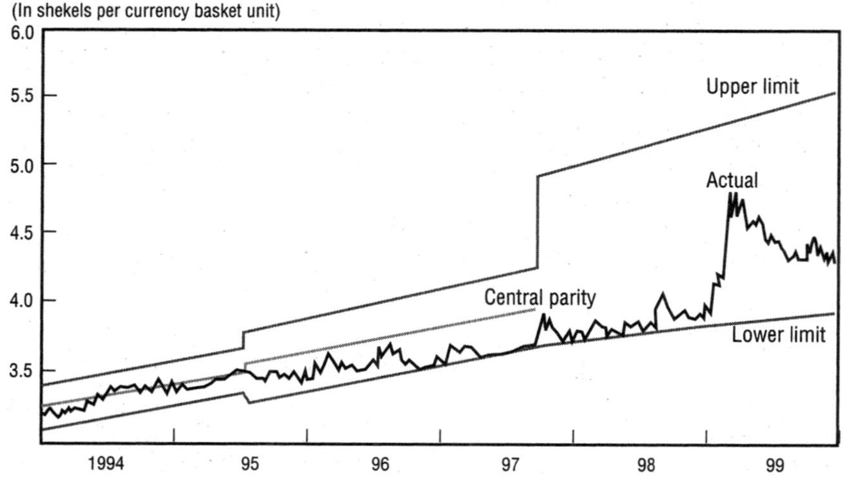

Source: Bank of Israel.

viations that occurred were quite minimal. Overall, then, from a multiyear perspective it can clearly be argued that inflation targets have been achieved on average: the average annual rate of inflation from 1992 to 1998 was 9.9 percent, which is very close to the average annual inflation target of 9.7 percent.

However, there were three major episodes of acceleration of inflation *within* years, to levels well above the target: these occurred in late 1994, in the first half of 1996, and in the last four months of 1998 (Figure 1). In all these cases, the regime was challenged and its credibility endangered, as revealed in the escalation of inflation expectations to about 15 percent per year in the first two episodes and to about 10 percent in the most recent episode. These circumstances created a situation where restrictive monetary policy was needed to counterbalance an expansionary fiscal policy and demand pressures in an overheated economy, and to reduce the implied deviation of the rate of inflation from the government's inflation target.

Figure 2 shows the evolution of Israel's nominal exchange rate against a basket of foreign currencies, and the evolution of the crawling exchange rate band. Like those of the inflation target, the parameters of the exchange rate regime are set by the government following consultation with the Bank of Israel. The crawling exchange rate band was introduced in late 1991, as a means of relaxing the fixity of the previous band system, which had been based on a fluctuation zone around a fixed central parity. The move to a more flexible system came after a series of speculative attacks on the shekel from 1988 to 1991; these attacks were mainly based on the perception that a fixed exchange rate was not sustainable in view of the persistent differential between domestic and foreign inflation. During this period the interest rate was used entirely to cope with speculative attacks on Israel's foreign currency reserves and not as an instrument for achieving a given inflation objective. From 1992 until late 1998 there were no major threats to the exchange rate regime, and the interest rate gradually took a central role in the effort to meet the inflation target. As noted previously, the inflation target was introduced for the first time in December 1991, as part of the new crawling band system.[4]

During the greater part of the crawling band's life span until 1996, the central bank operated an inner, intramarginal intervention band, aimed at keeping the exchange rate relatively close to the central parity. For several years capital inflows grew considerably, in part because of progress in the Middle East peace process from late 1993 onward, and in part as a result of financial opening and liberalization measures taken in previous years. The Bank of Israel purchased the considerable excess supply in the foreign exchange market, so that there was little change in the nominal exchange rate.

In late May 1995 the Bank of Israel and the Ministry of Finance announced the widening of the exchange rate band from 5 percent to 7 percent around the central parity rate. The initial purpose of this step was to adjust the exchange rate regime to allow for greater exchange rate flexibility. In spite of the potential increase in exchange rate risk, after a few weeks there was a strong tendency for the shekel to appreciate within the band, and the central bank returned to large-scale intervention in the foreign currency market. It is evident that market participants interpreted the perceived implicit commitment of the Bank of Israel to the inner band as a signal that there was little risk associated with exchange rate fluctuations. The combination of this perception and a sizable domestic-foreign interest rate differential provided an additional incentive for domestic agents to shift from domestic currency–denominated credit into borrowing abroad, thus strengthening short-term capital inflows and the pressure toward nominal appreciation of the currency. Overall, throughout the period between late 1994 and early 1998, the Bank of Israel purchased about $16 billion through foreign currency market intervention. The sterilization of these operations was carried out by eliminating monetary loans to the banking sector and creating deposits of the banking sector with the Bank of Israel (through a reverse repo).

---

[4]Specifically, the slope of the crawl (in annual terms) was set equal to the difference between the inflation target and a forecast of foreign inflation.

These developments, together with the objective to make further progress toward capital account liberalization and deepening of the foreign exchange market, prompted policy decisions that allowed for increased exchange rate flexibility. The inner band was abandoned in February 1996, providing more room for movements of the exchange rate within the band. By the summer of 1996 the shekel had appreciated to the band's lower limit. With capital inflows continuing to exert pressure for nominal appreciation, and given the desire to deepen the foreign exchange market and to make progress toward capital account convertibility, the next (and to date latest) change in the band's parameters occurred in June 1997. At that time additional room for exchange rate flexibility was introduced by enlarging the band width from 14 percent to 28 percent, to be gradually increased, from then until mid-1998, to 30 percent. The one-time increase in the band's width was implemented entirely by raising the upper (weaker) limit of the band. At the same time, the rate of crawl of the band's lower limit was reduced to 4 percent a year, but that of the upper limit was kept at 6 percent a year. The fact that the stock of foreign currency–denominated credit did not expand further in the second half of 1997 probably indicates a perception of greater exchange rate risk on the part of the private sector. This can be explained by the widening of the exchange rate band and by developments in foreign exchange markets in Asia. To a large extent, the reduction in foreign capital inflows was offset by a rise in foreign investment and by an improvement in the current account, resulting in the actual exchange rate remaining close to the lower limit of the band.

In sum, it seems that the very slow and gradual move toward increased flexibility of the nominal exchange rate, under conditions of considerable capital mobility and strong inflationary pressures, contributed to the conflict that monetary policy in Israel has faced over the last two to three years. That conflict has arisen from the need to support two nominal goals (the inflation target and the exchange rate band) with one instrument (the interest rate). The level of the interest rate required to meet the inflation target has been higher than that which would have resulted in no pressure on the exchange rate band limits. When those limits became a binding constraint, extensive sterilization of capital inflows was required—at a sizable quasi-fiscal cost—and monetary policy could not fully address inflation developments through the very important exchange rate channel of the monetary transmission mechanism.

The implications of the interaction between current and expected future developments on current monetary policy adjustments can be discussed in terms of developments in Israel (Figures 1 and 3). Figure 3 shows clearly that there have been three recent episodes of marked interest rate hikes by the central bank: in late 1994 and early 1995, in the second half of 1996, and in late

Figure 3

Israel: Inflation Expectations and Interest Rate on Bank of Israel Funds

(In percent per year)

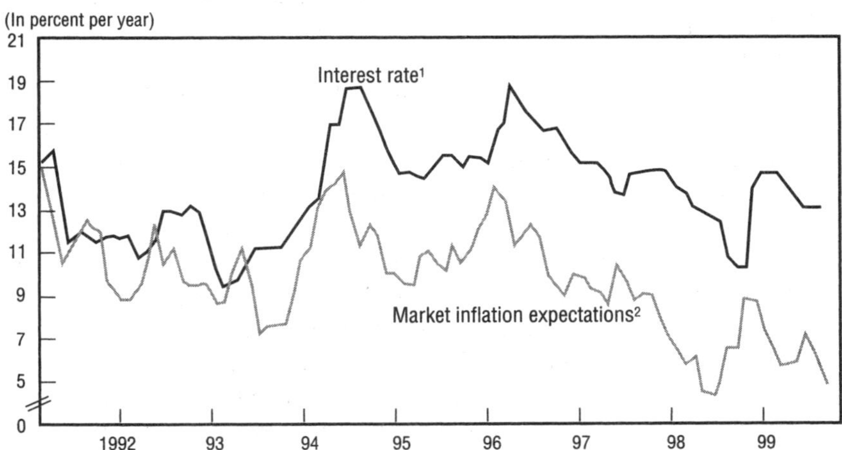

Source: Bank of Israel.
[1] Annualized effective rate on monetary loans by the Bank of Israel.
[2] Expectation of the rate of inflation 12 months ahead.

1998. Although there is no official or commonly used inflation forecast formulated by the Bank of Israel, market-based inflation expectations are widely used. In many cases these expectations, also plotted in Figure 3, have played a key role in Israel's inflation forecast targeting. The first two interest rate rises in Figure 3 were triggered by a combination of a rise in expected inflation, a rise in the government budget deficit, and a reduction in the rate of unemployment. The third was triggered by the turbulence in world financial markets in late 1998 and its implications for depreciation of the domestic currency. Along similar lines, when underlying factors signaled an easing of inflationary pressures, the central bank adjusted interest rates downward.

Policy Lessons

Israel's experience shares much in common with the experiences of other countries—in Asia, Eastern Europe, and Latin America—with similar or different nominal anchors. These commonalities allow some broad lessons and conclusions to be drawn.

First, although nominal exchange rate targeting has been extremely useful in the initial phase of a disinflation, as time has passed an increasing number of countries have found difficulties with this regime, especially under conditions of considerable capital mobility. The result has been a gradual move toward increased flexibility of nominal exchange rates. At the same time, official inflation targets have been taking more and more of the spotlight in monetary policymaking. Shifts in this direction have occurred, for example, in Sweden and in the United Kingdom in the early 1990s, and in Mexico and the Czech Republic more recently.

Second, the coexistence of multiple anchors—whether a crawling currency band together with an inflation target, or an inflation target together with a target for monetary aggregates—sooner or later becomes a source of policy conflict, which may damage policy credibility. For example, the use of high domestic real interest rates to combat inflation may be accompanied by substantial capital inflows, creating strong pressures for a nominal appreciation beyond the limit of the exchange rate band. This gives rise to the need for sterilized foreign exchange market intervention, which typically imposes a nonnegligible quasi-fiscal cost. In many other cases, high domestic real interest rates, required to defend the currency band in the face of demand for foreign exchange, could not be supported because they were higher than required for the planned disinflation.

Some of these difficulties can be reduced by setting a clear hierarchy of priorities between the two targets. Moreover, for those countries maintaining an exchange rate band, it is extremely important that the parameters of the two anchors be synchronized. For example, the slope of a crawling band needs to be synchronized with the inflation target.

Third, the extent to which the exchange rate is allowed to fluctuate, either within a band or in general through foreign exchange market intervention, has important side effects on the public's perception of exchange rate risk. This may give rise to a distortion, in the form of a perceived risk of exchange rate fluctuations that is much lower than is warranted in reality. This, in turn, may result in larger capital inflows and increased vulnerability. The main lesson here is that, if bands are used, they need to be broad enough not to create this distortion. True, this can result in greater exchange rate volatility, which can be damaging to some sectors, but this volatility can be attenuated by developing appropriate derivatives and other financial instruments.

Fourth, when inflation targets are used, it is extremely important to determine very clearly the principles of operation, mechanisms for ensuring accountability, the role of the central bank, and other functional and institutional details. To gain credibility, the inflation targeting regime has to be as unambiguous as possible. In addition, credibility is strengthened if there are supporting policies relating to the government budget, wages, and so forth, to avoid any overburdening of monetary policy. Synchronization of fiscal, monetary, and wage policies is extremely important for generating substantial reductions in inflation, as shown by the Israeli experience in 1991–92 and 1997–98.

The discretionary nature of inflation targets may lead to problems of credibility at the beginning of the regime. It is extremely important then how policy reacts. A strong and aggressive response, when needed, can generate credibility. In Israel, each of three major deviations of inflation from target was met by a strong policy reaction. Israel's experience shows that such a prompt reaction is key for gaining credibility.

References

Bruno, M., 1993, *Crisis, Stabilization and Economic Reform: Therapy by Consensus* (Oxford: Clarendon Press).

Bufman, G., L. Leiderman, and M. Sokoler, 1995, "Israel's Experience with Explicit Inflation Targets: A First Assessment," in *Inflation Targets*, ed. by L. Leiderman and L.E.O. Svensson (London: Centre for Economic Policy Research).

Helpman, E., L. Leiderman, and G. Bufman, 1994, "A New Breed of Exchange Rate Bands: Chile, Israel, and Mexico," *Economic Policy*, Vol. 19 (October), pp. 260–306.

Leiderman, L., 1993, *Inflation and Disinflation: The Israeli Experience* (Chicago: University of Chicago Press).

Leiderman, L., and G. Bufman, 1996, "Searching for Nominal Anchors in Shock-Prone Economies in the 1990s: Inflation Targets and Exchange Rate Bands," in *Securing Stability and Growth in Latin America: Policy Issues and Prospects for Shock-Prone Economies*, ed. by R. Hausmann and H. Reisen (Paris: Organisation for Economic Co-operation and Development).

Leiderman, L., and Lars E.O. Svensson, eds., 1995, *Inflation Targets* (London: Centre for Economic Policy Research).

Sokoler, Meir, 1997, "Credibility Half-Won in an Ongoing Battle: An Analysis of Inflation Targets and Monetary Policy in Israel," Working Paper prepared jointly with members of the Monetary Department, Bank of Israel (Jerusalem).

10 Mexico's Monetary Policy Framework Under a Floating Exchange Rate Regime

Agustín G. Carstens and Alejandro M. Werner[1]

The recent currency and financial crises in emerging markets have reignited the debate on viable exchange rate regimes for small, open economies. One common element in all of these crises was the adherence to a predetermined exchange rate. Thus, several analysts have concluded that only under very specific and demanding conditions might there be a comfortable middle ground between a floating exchange rate and the adoption of a common currency. In Latin America this polarization in the choice of exchange rate regimes is clearly represented by the different paths taken by Argentina and Mexico. After more than four years of experience with a floating exchange rate regime, Mexico provides an interesting case study for other emerging economies considering moving toward a more flexible exchange rate regime.

A Forced Transition to Floating: 1994–95

The fragilities that accumulated in the Mexican economy during the early 1990s and the negative shocks the country faced during 1994 culminated in the balance of payments and financial crisis of December 1994. The crisis had three different dimensions. The first was a current account deficit of significant proportions, generated by domestic overspending and financed by short-run capital inflows. The second was the equivalent of a run on Mexican external liabilities, both government and private. The third was the banking crisis that then began to unfold, which required immediate attention both to avoid a domestic run on the banks and to pursue consistency in the macroeconomic

---

[1]The views expressed in this paper are the sole responsibility of the authors and do not necessarily represent those of the institutions with which they are affiliated.

framework. To confront these three challenges, several measures were implemented during 1995:

- Monetary and fiscal policies were tightened.

- The government negotiated a $52 billion international support package.

- The authorities implemented a series of programs to prevent a systemic run on the banking system, combat moral hazard, minimize distortions, and strengthen financial sector regulation and supervision.

The key to Mexico's success in stabilizing relatively quickly was the adoption of a consistent macroeconomic program immediately after the crisis. In particular, the fiscal authority, by recognizing the costs of restructuring the banking sector and by showing its commitment to deal with this problem with fiscal resources, liberated monetary policy to pursue its primary goal of price stability.

Monetary Policy Since 1995

The devaluation of the peso and the return to high inflation in 1995 seriously damaged the credibility of the Bank of Mexico. Yet having abandoned using the exchange rate as the economy's nominal anchor, monetary policy had no choice but to fill the vacuum.

First, to keep inflation in line, the Bank of Mexico established as an intermediate target a ceiling on the growth of the monetary base for the year. Unfortunately, it soon became obvious that this simple monetary program was not enough to stabilize inflationary expectations, the exchange rate, or inflation itself. In early 1995 the rule-based monetary policy failed to perform as expected, for several reasons:

- In a crisis scenario, the velocity of money becomes very unstable.

- The rule on growth of the monetary base was unable to keep the sudden depreciation of the peso from affecting inflationary expectations and the price level.

- The central bank had hardly any control over the monetary base in the short run.

This experience led the Mexican authorities to modify their monetary policy, from one based solely on quantitative targets on monetary aggregates to one using a combination of rules (on the behavior of the monetary base) and discretion (by influencing the level of interest rates).

To be able to implement the discretionary policy measures transparently, the central bank decided to adopt a zero *average* reserve requirement. Under this scheme, the Bank of Mexico established accounting periods of 28 days, during which banks would be given incentives to post a zero average daily balance in the current accounts they hold at the central bank. Should a bank's average daily balance become negative, the bank would have to pay a penalty interest rate equivalent to twice the prevailing 28-day rate on CETES (bills issued by the Mexican treasury) on the balance. On the other hand, a positive daily average balance would mean that the bank was forgoing the returns it could have obtained had it invested those funds in the market.

To meet the demand for bills and coins, the Bank of Mexico offers credit to banks in daily auctions, so as to offset maturing credits previously granted to the banks, movements in the account of the national treasury, and the monetary impact of the central bank's transactions in foreign currency. The central bank determines the sum of credit to be auctioned each day, so that the overall net average daily balance of all current accounts held by banks at the central bank—accumulated during the specific 28-day accounting period—will close the day at a predetermined amount. If that amount is negative, the central bank puts the banking system in a "short" position; if positive, the system is put in a "long" position. It follows that if the central bank puts the system in the "short" position, at least one credit institution will have to pay the penalty interest rate.

It should be stressed that the Bank of Mexico always supplies the credit necessary to completely satisfy demand for bills and coins, even when the banking system is "short." But in such cases a portion of the credit is supplied at a higher interest rate, which is applied to the overdrafts in the current accounts of one or several banks. When the system is "short," the central bank exerts upward pressure on interest rates, which can be quite significant but is primarily the result of the signal given by the Bank of Mexico.

Since 1996, all the monetary programs that the Bank of Mexico has implemented have included three main elements:

- A yearly annual inflation objective;

- A rules-defined base, together with quantitative commitments on the accumulation of net international reserves and the variation of net domestic credit; and

- The possibility for the central bank to adjust its stance on monetary policy, should unexpected circumstances make it advisable (this element represents the use of discretion in monetary policy management).

The central bank tends to use the "short" mechanism, thereby adopting a more restrictive stance, when it detects future inflationary pressures that are inconsistent with the attainment of the inflationary target, when it is deemed necessary to restore order in foreign exchange and money markets, or when inflationary expectations are deemed out of line with respect to the original target.

In order to design a suitable monetary policy framework, it is essential to identify the main determinants of inflation and understand how monetary policy interacts with them to affect the rate of increase of the consumer price index (CPI). There are two alternative explanations of the source of inflationary pressures. In the first, the traditional monetary explanation, exogenous shocks to the supply of money cause inflation. In the second, based on models that assume price rigidities, shocks to key prices in the economy (wages, the exchange rate, or prices of public sector output) affect inflation directly, and monetary policy partially accommodates these shocks. In this scenario, the degree of policy accommodation is instrumental in determining the long-run inflationary impact of the shock.

A close look at trends in the growth rate of the monetary base and inflation during 1986–98 indicates that changes in inflation have preceded changes in the growth rate of base money. This suggests that, during this period, exogenous movements in the money stock were not the fundamental cause of inflation. Results of Granger causality tests show causality running both ways between these two variables. However, these results do not quantify the influence that movements in either of these variables had on the other. To analyze this issue in more detail, we estimated a vector error correction model that incorporates, as its endogenous variables, the CPI, base money, the exchange rate, wages, and public sector prices.

The results of the variance decomposition exercises confirm that exogenous movements in the monetary base have not been a cause of inflationary pressures, but rather that the money base has accommodated inflationary shocks coming from the exchange rate, wages, and public sector prices. These results imply that discretionary policy measures (or reactions) to combat shocks should be the main component of Mexico's monetary program. So it is safe to assume that inflationary pressures in Mexico have their origin in nonmonetary factors (validated ex post by the monetary authority). These include external shocks, which may generate a sharp depreciation of the currency; changes in public sector prices; and wage revisions that are inconsistent with the inflation target.

Confronted with these exogenous inflationary shocks, the central bank must decide whether to accommodate their inflationary impact through its monetary policy actions, and if so, whether totally or partially. To understand the problems that the central bank faces, it is convenient to analyze first the case where some accommodation is made to these shocks.

Consider the case where an exogenous shock causes a sharp nominal depreciation of the currency. If this depreciation is perceived as permanent, it will soon translate into increases in tradable goods prices, generating a higher CPI. This, in turn, increases nominal demand for money. If the central bank passively matches the demand and the supply of base money, this expansion will be validated, and the central bank will have accommodated the increase in money demand. An economics textbook would describe this as a once-and-for-all adjustment in the price level, which should be accommodated.

However, in a country with a history of high inflation, the dynamics triggered by such a depreciation are more complicated. The public might be led to revise their expectations of future inflation upward, and this would lead to rises in wages and nontradable goods prices, and thus to subsequent rounds of exchange rate and wage adjustments.

The central bank should be able to offset at least part of the inflationary impact of such an exogenous shock to the exchange rate (or to public sector prices or contractual wages). It can do so, for example, by satisfying the daily monetary base demand, but at an interest rate above that prevailing in the market. This is, in fact, what happens when the Bank of Mexico puts banks in "short" or increases the short position. The resulting higher interest rates may, for example, partly reverse the impact of an exogenous exchange rate shock, limiting the depreciation and moderating the adjustment of inflationary expectations. In fact, this was the Bank of Mexico's attitude during 1998 and 1999, when it increased the short position on several occasions as additional inflationary shocks became apparent.

Exchange Rate Policy Since 1995

The exchange rate of the Mexican peso has been floating freely since late 1994. From time to time since then, the need has arisen for various reasons for the authorities to intervene in the foreign exchange market. In all such cases, the authorities have followed the rule that their intervention must be completely transparent, and without defending a particular level of the exchange rate.

As already mentioned, one of the most important elements of the 1994–95 crisis was the run on the country's external liabilities. On the public sector side, the run concentrated on the now-famous *tesobonos,* which are short-term dollar-denominated government securities. In the private sector, commercial banks faced difficulties in rolling over their external liabilities. Even after the international assistance package was approved, the resources were made available, and the adjustment program was in place, relatively large amortizations of *tesobonos* and bank credits continued. It soon became obvious that if the excess demand for foreign exchange that generated this abrupt stock adjustment in the holdings of Mexican liabilities was not satisfied by official intervention, a sharp depreciation could ensue, even raising the risk of hyperinflation.

In addition, in the wake of the crisis, Mexico faced the need to rebuild its international reserves. This had to be done, moreover, without affecting the floating exchange rate and without sending any signals to the market that might be interpreted as reflecting a desired level for the exchange rate. To accomplish this task, the Bank of Mexico implemented auctions of dollar put options.

On several occasions under the floating exchange rate regime when the peso has depreciated sharply, liquidity in the foreign exchange markets has almost dried up. Under such circumstances, small changes in the demand for foreign currency have led to disproportionate depreciations of the peso. These conditions might lead to a devaluatory spiral, which could seriously affect inflation and interest rates. To moderate these extreme situations, a contingent dollar sales scheme was introduced in February 1997.

Given the macroeconomic framework that has been maintained during the period of floating exchange rates, the exchange rate regime has not been an impediment to achieving a rapid disinflation: inflation fell from 51.7 percent in 1995 to 18.6 percent in 1998. The volatility experienced by the peso during its float, once the macroeconomic and financial crises were contained, has been similar to that experienced by other currencies with floating exchange rates.

As a simple test of the effects of the different exchange rate regimes on interest rate levels and volatilities, we can compare the behavior of interest rates in the 1996–99 period with that observed during 1989–94, when the performance of inflation was similar. In the current stabilization effort, under a floating exchange rate, interest rates have usually been lower and less volatile than during the years of the Economic Solidarity Pact (1987–94), when a predetermined exchange rate was in place.

In Mexico's experience, the adoption of a floating exchange rate regime has contributed substantially to reducing speculative pressures in financial markets. A very important feature of this regime is that it discourages short-term capital flows, because of the risk to investors of large losses from exchange rate fluctuations in the short run.

The flexible exchange rate also facilitates the adjustment of the real exchange rate toward equilibrium whenever an external shock warrants a new equilibrium real exchange rate, without seriously harming the credibility of the monetary authority. These movements in the real exchange rate are useful to minimize the effects of external shocks on the economy. However, given Mexico's history of high inflation, inflation expectations react immediately when the peso depreciates. Therefore, the inflation cost of achieving the necessary correction in the real exchange rate has been significantly higher than in other countries.

Conclusion

The recent crises in financial markets underscore the importance of maintaining a consistent macroeconomic framework, whatever the choice of exchange rate regime, so as to avoid financial and balance of payments crises and achieve long-lasting stability. It is clear that assigning multiple objectives to a single monetary policy instrument has led to the collapse of several regimes based on fixed or at least predetermined exchange rates. Therefore one of the most important steps that Mexico undertook after the collapse of the peso was to spell out clearly that monetary policy was going to be focused exclusively on attaining its medium-run goal of price stability. Also important was communicating the determination that the banking sector problem was going to be addressed by specific programs, whose cost the fiscal authority would assume.

The floating exchange rate regime has not proved to be an obstacle to Mexico's efforts to disinflate. On the contrary, it has contributed significantly to the adjustment of the economy to external shocks and to discouraging short-term capital inflows. Thus the floating exchange rate has become a very important element of Mexico's current macroeconomic policy framework.

11 Issues in the Adoption of an Inflation Targeting Framework in Brazil

Research Department, Central Bank of Brazil[1]

Since the 1980s there has been a growing consensus worldwide on the importance of price stability as the overriding long-term objective for monetary policy. This consensus stems in part from the fact that monetary policy can produce effects in the real economy only in the short run. Expansionary monetary policy may lead to higher levels of employment and economic activity, but only until businesses and workers start to react, adjusting their price and wage expectations accordingly. Thereafter the only result is higher inflation, with no output gains. More recently, empirical evidence has shown a negative correlation between high inflation and economic growth, suggesting that the best goal for monetary policy is to promote price stability.

Meanwhile the loss of public confidence in policy regimes that target monetary aggregates or the exchange rate has forced central banks to look for a more credible nominal anchor. Many have recently adopted explicit inflation targeting as their monetary policy regime. Now Brazil is joining the club: the Central Bank of Brazil intends to put in place a formal inflation targeting framework as rapidly as is feasible.

Macroeconomic Background

The stabilization program initiated in Brazil in mid-1994 successfully brought annual inflation down to single-digit figures in less than three years. This program included a wide range of economic reforms: many state enterprises were privatized; trade liberalization was deepened through reductions in import

---

[1]This paper reflects the views of the Research Department of the Central Bank of Brazil but not necessarily those of its directors.

tariffs and elimination of nontariff trade barriers; prudential regulation of the financial system was updated; and unsound financial institutions were liquidated. Real output growth averaged 3.4 percent per year in 1994–98, although unemployment started to rise in 1997. Despite its success, the stabilization process involved a gradualist approach to many structural economic problems, which remained unsolved after several years. A much-needed definitive fiscal adjustment was continually postponed because a consensus on its urgency could not be reached in the congress.

Therefore Brazil remained vulnerable to a confidence crisis, which became a reality when the international financial turmoil that began in East Asia culminated in the Russian debt moratorium in August 1998. The resulting crisis of confidence generated massive capital flight from emerging markets. In response, Brazil raised short-term interest rates and announced strong fiscal tightening measures. At the same time, Brazil negotiated with the International Monetary Fund a preventive financial support package totaling $41.5 billion. The government was initially successful in implementing elements of the fiscal package, but market confidence continued to weaken in January 1999. This in part reflected concerns about the weak commitment of some large Brazilian states to adjusting their finances. Following strong pressures on foreign exchange reserves, on January 15 the Brazilian currency, the real, was allowed to float. The exchange rate averaged 1.52 reals to the dollar in January and 1.91 to the dollar in February, compared with 1.21 to the dollar before the change in regime. This led private analysts to foresee a huge deterioration in all macroeconomic fundamentals, but these projections were so exaggerated that they had to be reviewed less than two months later.

Inflation rose sharply until March. Wholesale prices (as measured by the IPA-DI/FGV) rose 7.0 percent in February, but only 2.8 percent in March; rates of consumer price inflation (as measured by the IPC-DI/FGV) were 1.4 percent and 0.9 percent in the same months. This deceleration in prices was mainly due to a reversal, at the beginning of March, of the exchange rate overshooting that had occurred during the crisis. After the initial excessive depreciation of the real, prices of tradable goods soared, but not in the same proportion. The pass-through to consumer prices was much less than could have been anticipated. Brazilian consumers had gotten used to stable prices, and when retail prices started to rise too quickly, the decline in demand was immediate. This reaction forced price negotiations between clients and suppliers, which resulted in a dilution of the devaluation effects throughout the production chain.

Economic activity in 1999 is now expected to recover sooner than projected a few months ago, with GDP declining by only 1–2 percent on average for the year. This reflects a pronounced downturn of activity in the second half of 1998, and a likely further decline in domestic demand in the first half of 1999, which will be only partly offset by a recovery of net exports. The economic downturn is expected to bottom out around the second quarter, with a gradual recovery beginning thereafter and gathering momentum in 2000, as confidence recovers, external financing constraints are eased, and real interest rates decline.

The shift to a floating exchange rate will require a new nominal anchor for economic policy. Monetary policy, along with strengthened fiscal adjustment and a firm wage policy in the public sector, will be instrumental in preventing the recurrence of an inflationary spiral and ensuring a rapid deceleration of inflation. The consumer price index may still rise in the second quarter of 1999, but its rate of increase should then taper off, reflecting the firm stance of monetary policy and the absence of domestic demand pressures.

The depreciation of the real, through its impact on the external and foreign exchange–indexed domestic public debt, in particular, boosted the total public debt to 52 percent of GDP in March 1999. The government intends to steadily reduce the ratio of the public debt to GDP to less than 50 percent by the end of 1999, and to less than 46 percent by the end of 2001. This will be accomplished through higher-than-originally-targeted primary surpluses of the consolidated public sector in the next three years. The pursuit of this objective should also be helped by a decline of real interest rates, expected to result from the implementation of the inflation targeting framework, strengthened fiscal adjustment, and the move to a floating exchange rate regime. Projections of the debt-GDP ratio under plausible assumptions about GDP growth, real interest rates, and the real exchange rate suggest that primary surpluses of 3 percent of GDP in each year during the period 1999–2001 should be sufficient for this purpose.

Nevertheless, to build in a safety margin in the event the environment is less favorable than projected, the government has increased the targeted primary surplus to at least 3.1 percent of GDP in 1999, 3.2 percent of GDP in 2000, and 3.3 percent of GDP in 2001. The fiscal results for the consolidated public sector in the first two months of 1999—a primary surplus of 3.7 percent of GDP—far exceeded the objective.

Structural reforms will continue. Passage of the proposed Fiscal Responsibility Law will be given high priority. This law provides the backdrop for attaining the primary surpluses required to stabilize the debt-GDP ratio. The government also intends to accelerate and further broaden the scope of its privatization program, completing the privatization of the federal electric power generating companies and, beginning in 2000, the privatization of the transmission network. The legislative framework for the privatization or leasing of water and sewage utilities is being prepared.

Issues of Design and Implementation

Designing and implementing the inflation targeting regime requires addressing a number of technical issues, and several preconditions must be met if the regime is to be successful.

Defining Price Stability

Strictly speaking, price stability means that the *price level* remains constant, that is, that the inflation rate is zero. But this is not what economists and central bankers usually have in mind when they talk about price stability. Fischer (1996) argues that the government should pursue an average rate of annual inflation centered at 2 percent, with a tolerance interval of plus or minus 1 percent. Most of the industrial countries that have adopted inflation targeting aim at midpoints of 3 percent or less.

Inflation is socially undesirable, so why do central banks not pursue a zero inflation target? The main reason is the technical difficulty of measuring inflation with complete accuracy. Inflation rates calculated from consumer price indices are subject to an upward measurement bias, so that when measured inflation equals zero, actual inflation is negative. And because economists have well-justified fears of deflation, they typically consider it prudent to target a modestly positive rate of measured inflation. Theoretical reasons can also be found for erring on the positive side. When inflation is zero, real interest rates cannot be negative. But negative real interest rates can be a powerful instrument for economic recovery during a recession. Moreover, when nominal prices have downward rigidities, as is common with wages, a positive inflation rate allows real wages to decline after an unfavorable shock hits the economy, thus reducing the necessary adjustment costs.

Defining the Inflation Targeting Regime

An inflation targeting regime can be defined as a strategy for conducting monetary policy with the overriding and explicit objective of achieving and maintaining price stability, represented by an easily understandable, numerical target value for inflation. Given this target, the central bank is typically allowed flexibility to choose the combination of monetary policy instrument settings it judges most appropriate to achieve the objective, based on the most complete information available. These decisions are announced and explained to the public, thus increasing the transparency of monetary policy. As an obvious counterpart, the central bank is made accountable for attaining the inflation goal.

Preconditions for Inflation Targeting in Brazil

One of the crucial elements of a successful inflation targeting regime is the use of inflation forecasts as the main intermediate variable that guides decisions on instrument settings. In order to apply such a forward-looking procedure, the central bank must have adequate knowledge about the way the economy works. That is, it ought to be able to model the monetary policy transmission mechanism with, at least, a sufficient degree of accuracy to correctly assess inflationary pressures and the implications of consequent decisions for instrument setting. Therefore the central bank staff must have adequate technical skills to extract the correct signals from the available information.

However, the main challenges of inflation targeting are not technical, but rather relate to institutional and macroeconomic features. The basic precondition to implementing an inflation targeting regime is operational independence for the central bank in the conduct of monetary policy. Here, the word *independence* means that no factor other than inflation should condition monetary policy decisions. The presence of fiscal dominance, for example, is incompatible with instrument independence.

Brazil fulfills all the preconditions for adopting an inflation targeting regime. The Central Bank of Brazil already enjoys a high degree of operational autonomy. Since 1996 the Monetary Policy Committee, whose members are the central bank directors, has been solely responsible for setting basic short-term interest rates. This autonomy has been clearly confirmed at several critical moments. For example, after the Russian crisis in August 1998, the central bank did not hesitate to adjust interest rates upward, even though a presidential election campaign was under way. Fiscal policy had to be adjusted accordingly, given the immediate rise in interest payments on the public debt. This provided strong evidence of "monetary dominance" rather than fiscal dominance.

The government has a broad revenue base—total public sector receipts exceed 30 percent of GDP—and hence does not depend on seigniorage. Domestic financial markets are sophisticated and deep enough to finance the public debt on their own. Nonetheless, it is recognized that the nominal fiscal deficit should be reduced, and this is exactly what the fiscal adjustment program mentioned above intends to accomplish. The first results for 1999 have shown that the proposed fiscal targets are achievable and that the government's determination to achieve them is indisputable.

Today, Brazil has a floating exchange rate regime; therefore monetary policy can be used for the sole purpose of hitting the inflation targets. In addition, the change in the exchange rate regime proved to be less traumatic than initially expected. The exchange rate is already returning to a stable equilibrium, and estimates of consumer price inflation for 1999 are below 10 percent, far less than previously expected.

A Proposal for Brazil

As there are presently no indications of an inflationary process in Brazil, a gradualist disinflation strategy is not recommended: consumer price inflation should return to its 1998 level (1.7 percent) as soon as the relative price realignment is complete. Thus it is not only possible but also desirable for the government to set a low inflation target to be achieved in 2000. The combination of very high domestic interest rates, fiscal tightening, and the floating of the currency may lead to negative output growth in 1999. Conditions are now very favorable for bringing down interest rates while at the same time achieving lower inflation and higher output growth.

Although Brazil is in a transition period toward a steady state, it should set either a target ceiling for inflation or a target that is surrounded by an asymmetric tolerance interval. Thus, for 1999, our estimates indicate that a reasonable target value is an inflation rate, in terms of the full consumer price index, of 10 percent, which is high enough to provide room for the realignment of relative prices. The target for 2000 should be around 5 percent, with a tolerance interval of plus or minus 2 percentage points. These are only tentative numbers, but they are in line with both the accumulated inflation already verified in 1999 and the official pronouncements of the finance minister since the floating of the real. Both targets should be announced simultaneously by mid-1999.

There is a near consensus that targets should be set in terms of the inflation rate, not in terms of the price level. The targets should be set by the finance minister in a first implementation scheme. The central bank will then be accountable to the finance ministry for hitting the target. Any failures will have to be publicly justified in an open letter.

There will initially be a tolerance interval of 2 percentage points around the established target. This range is justified by the forecasting ability of the different models during the initial inflation targeting period, and it accounts for uncertainties about the structural changes that will result from the new arrangements. An effective public communication process will be established so that Brazilian society will be able to understand and monitor the decisions of the central bank and know the reasons why forecast and accumulated inflation are deviating from the target, should that occur.

The central bank will consider a mix of models as it looks for an adequate reaction function and produces inflation forecasts and their probability distributions. Decisions about monetary policy should be made on the basis of the broadest information set available, including indicators of private sector perceptions about the expected path of economic variables, information about variables outside the model, information about leading indicators, and any other judgmental knowledge that will help in predicting inflation.

As to the choice of a price index, there is no doubt that Brazil should target a rate of consumer price inflation, not only because it is a good measure of welfare, but also because it is already well known and easily understood by the public. There are, however, different consumer price indices regularly published in Brazil. A good choice might be the IPC-DI, published by the Fundação Getúlio Vargas, an independent institution whose credibility is unquestioned. Other indices, such as the IPCA and the INPC, would be even more appropriate, because they cover a wider range of cities and incomes. But they have some important disadvantages: they are calculated by a government institution (the Instituto Brasileiro de Geografia e Estatistica, the government's statistical institute), and they lack a regular publication schedule.

Another important issue is whether to target the full or "headline" inflation rate or some measure of core inflation. Technically, the best approach would be to purge some items from the full price index, to eliminate the effects of temporary and once-and-for-all shocks. Failure of the full index to abstract from these effects may worsen the medium-term inflation path, threatening the success of monetary policy. But reasons of credibility make adoption of a full index essential. Unfortunately, Brazilian society has witnessed several manipulations of price indices, both in the relatively distant past and more recently, and therefore would be suspicious about any suggestion to suppress items from the target index.

The Monetary Policy Committee will be responsible for setting values of monetary policy instruments, especially short-term interest rates. The formal arrangements will essentially remain unchanged. The committee will meet at regular five-week intervals, and decisions will be made by majority vote. These decisions will be announced immediately after the meeting, together with a press release explaining briefly the reasons for the decisions. The minutes of the meetings will be published 15 days thereafter.

Finally, an inflation report will be published quarterly, discussing the main issues related to the performance of the inflation targeting regime. The report will include detailed explanations of the results of past decisions as well as prospective analyses, with special emphasis on the assumptions made in the forecasting process that generated the monetary instrument decisions. Minutes of previous Monetary Policy Committee meetings will be included as well.

Reference

Fischer, Stanley, 1996, "Why Are Central Banks Pursuing Long-Run Price Stability?" in *Achieving Price Stability* (Kansas City, Missouri: Federal Reserve Bank of Kansas City).